DADDY DOIN' WORK

Empowering Mothers to Evolve Fatherhood

For information on subsidiary rights, please contact the publisher at rights@jollyfishpress.com. For a complete list of our wholesalers and distributors, please visit our website at www.jollyfishpress.com.

For information, write us at Jolly Fish Press, PO Box 1773, Provo, UT 84603-1773.

Printed in the United States of America

THIS TITLE IS ALSO AVAILABLE AS AN EBOOK.

Library of Congress Cataloging-in-Publication Data

Richards, Doyin, 1974-
 Daddy doin' work : empowering mothers to evolve fatherhood / Doyin Richards. -- First paperback edition.
     pages cm
 Summary: "Doyin Richards' adventures in fatherhood have been documented on his blog, Daddy Doin' Work. With this book, he answers questions about fatherhood that many women want to know in his no-nonsense, entertaining style. He urges new mothers to enter the minds of new dads, thereby changing their perception of what should be expected from a modern father. Richards exposes the manipulative secrets of deadbeat dads, offers practical tips to help hardworking dads understand that being a father encompasses more than paying the bills, and provides methods to ensure that amazing dads stay on track while inspiring more fathers to be just like them. Most importantly, women will be forced to take a long look in the mirror to determine if they are part of the solution or part of the problem in shaping the behavior of modern fathers"-- Provided by publisher.
 Summary: "Empowers mothers to make smart relationship decisions by entering the minds of fathers to change the perception of what should be expected from a modern father"--Provided by publisher"-- Provided by publisher.
 ISBN 978-1-63163-014-9 (paperback)
1. Fatherhood--United States. 2. Father and child--United States. 3. Mothers--United States. 4. Parenting--United States. 5. Child care--United States. I. Title.
 HQ756.R49 2014
  306.874'2--dc23
                              2014026827

10 9 8 7 6 5 4 3 2 1

For my daughters Emiko and Reiko:

Not a day passes when I don't thank my lucky stars for letting me be the primary male influence in your lives. Any good dad will tell his kids that being a good role model is a huge responsibility, and it's one I take very seriously. I don't know a lot of things, but I know for a fact that I was born to be your daddy. As you grow older, I hope you know that everything about my mission is centered around, and inspired by, both of you. Thank you for making me a better man. I love you to infinity and back.

PRAISES FOR DADDY DOIN' WORK

"This is a down to earth, straight- shooting, and humorous depiction of what fatherhood often is, as well as what it could and should be!"
—Alan Blankstein, award-winning author of *Failure Is Not an Option*

"I am many things in this life: son, brother, athlete, lover, fighter, actor, producer, writer,etc. But the first word I use to describe myself and the job I take most pride in is the role of DAD. Doyin takes this role as seriously as I do, and he writes in a very conversational and straightforward way that makes you feel like you're sharing coffee with him, not reading his book. A must-read for all modern fathers."
—Dean Cain, actor, producer, and dad

"I wish every father could parent in the same modern and supportive way that Doyin does. His book is something every new and expecting dad could benefit from and every new mom will be eternally grateful for!"
—Jill Smokler, Scary Mommy, and New York Times best-selling author of *Confessions of a Scary Mommy* and *Motherhood Comes Naturally (And Other Vicious Lies)*

"Doyin created a really important book that talks about the ways in which men are evolving and changing in the twenty-first century. He masters the combination of being informative, casual, insightful and entertaining, all while making you feel like you are sitting in a room having a conversation with him."
—Lisa Hickey, CEO of The Good Men Project

DOYIN RICHARDS

DADDY DOIN' WORK
Empowering Mothers to Evolve Fatherhood

JOLLY
FISH
PRESS
Provo, Utah

INTRODUCTION

"WHAT DO YOU WANT TO be when you grow up?"

I remember when I was in fourth grade and my teacher asked the class that very question. With a few exceptions, every girl wanted to be a veterinarian, teacher, nurse, or a mother. The boys in our class were equally as predictable, as many wanted to be professional athletes, police officers, firefighters, or astronauts.

Then there was me.

I wanted to be a rapper. Not only did I think I'd make big bucks with my rhymes, but I also came to class prepared to share my skills with everyone. Mind you, the assignment was only to share the name of the profession and offer a quick synopsis as to why we would want to pursue it. No chance I was following those rules. This was going to be my big break. Because, hey, in my knuckleheaded mind, the not-so-mean streets of suburban Amherst, Massachusetts, were crawling with hip-hop record producers who would line up to sign "MC D-Rich" (yes, that was my stage name. Don't ask).

When it was my turn to present in front of the class, I shared my "Cafeteria" rap with them. Feel free to add your own beat box in the background.

The cafeteria is an awful place.
Food smells good, but has no taste.

Soggy burgers and greasy fries
Made a few tears come to my eyes.

I called my friend to see my plate,
And he said, "Hold on there, you better wait"

Why should I wait? Why should I look?
Because the food on my plate ain't fully cooked.

And then I jumped back—and to my surprise,
The thing on my plate just opened its eyes!

I remember folding my arms like the cool kids did back in the 80s and waited for a response from the class. After about seven seconds of awkward silence, my teacher forced a smile. "Thank you, Doyin. Please have a seat. Okay, who would like to go next?"

That moment crushed my rap career before it ever got off of the ground, and that's a damn good thing for everyone involved. However, one thing happened that day that went completely unnoticed until I grew up: some of the girls mentioned they wanted to become moms, but not one of the boys said they wanted to become dads.

Even at young ages, kids are force-fed society's lines about what they should do for a living. Boys should do "manly" things that will help provide a good life for their wives and children. In other words, find a way to get (and keep) a good job that pays a good salary. I bought into that formula. Pretty much every dude I know bought into it. The irony isn't lost upon me, because I now know that there's no better way for a man to provide a good life for his wife and children than being a good, involved dad and a committed parenting partner to his spouse.

The first little boy I come across who says his goal in life is to become a dad when he grows up will be the first. Why?

Because many boys and young men don't equate being a dad to being something that requires work.

Becoming a lawyer requires work. Becoming a professional basketball player requires work. Becoming a doctor requires work. Hell, even becoming a rapper requires work. Not only do those professions require work, they also pay damn good money. What's the salary for being a good dad these days? Exactly.

Being a good dad requires work, too. A shitload of work. Work that is often tedious, exhausting, and frustrating. Work that will not pay a man a dime for the amount of time he puts into changing diapers, giving baths, helping with homework, being a shoulder to cry on, being an active and willing parenting partner with his spouse, and being the primary male role model in his kids' lives.

However, it's easily the most rewarding work a man can do, and nobody can put a price tag on it.

It starts with the toothless infant smiles when his baby looks at him, and it continues until he receives the "TYT" and beyond. By the way, the TYT is the "Thank You Talk." It's that point in a dad's life when his kids are old enough to say, "You know when you were a hard ass to me growing up, and I kept telling you that I hated you? Well, now I know why you did those things. Thank you for being such a great dad."

My dad received the TYT from my two brothers and me, and to this day he lists those conversations as some of the proudest moments since he became a father. He put in work at his day job prior to retiring. He puts in work as a devoted husband to my mom as they celebrate forty-four years of marriage and counting. When we were younger, he put in work as an amazing parenting partner that helped my mom survive dealing with three crazy little boys during her time as a stay-at-home mom. He puts in work by always showing my two brothers and me that no matter what he had going on in his life being a dad to us was (and still is) his main priority. Whenever we talk, he always tells me that his hard work paid off.

The key word in there is *work*. My dad is always doin' work for our family, and that earns him the title of a Daddy Doin' Work. Yes, that phrase rolls off the tongue easier than the drool from the mouth of my teething baby girl, but it's intended to be more than something catchy and cute. It's intended to be the gold standard that all dads should strive to become if they aren't there already.

Are we there yet?

Are you kidding me? Turn on your televisions and you'll see modern dads depicted as bumbling buffoons who don't know their asses from their elbows when it comes to childcare. On a personal level, not a day goes by when I don't receive emails from exasperated moms fed up with the lack of support at home from their men. With the same frequency, I also receive emails from amazing dads who are frustrated by the women in their lives trying to micromanage how they raise their kids. At least once a week I see moms losing their minds in excitement over dads completing simple parenting tasks they can do in their sleep.

So, no. We're not there yet.

Can we get there someday?

Absolutely, we can. But we need to approach the problem from a different angle, and that angle is to empower women to evolve fatherhood. Confused? Don't sweat it. It will all make perfect sense once you dive into the book. I'm not a parenting expert—and let's face it, neither are you. There's no such thing as a parenting expert; however, I know my shit when it comes to dads (whether they are crappy, mediocre, or excellent). Just think of me as your tour guide as we take the scenic route to understanding what evolving fatherhood is all about.

You already paid for your tour ticket by owning this book. So buckle your seatbelt, get comfortable, and make sure you use the potty before we drive down this extremely important road. Nothing is more annoying than asking your passengers if they need to pee before you leave the house, and then ten minutes later little Susie is complaining about an urgent need to tinkle. Don't be Susie.

I digress.

Ready? Let's go.

CHAPTER 1
WHEN I BROKE THE INTERNET

SINCE WE'RE GOING TO BECOME acquainted on this long journey, I probably should let you in on a personal secret before we hit the road:

I broke the Internet.

Yes, you read that correctly. Not too long ago I personally demolished everything that Al Gore worked so tirelessly to build. The result wasn't due to creating a super virus that wreaked havoc upon the worlds' computers. It was simply due to a photo and a blog post. A photo and a blog post that clearly illustrate why we need to evolve fatherhood in the first place.

THE BACKSTORY

Let's rewind back to when my youngest daughter, Reiko (Ray-Coe), was three months old and my oldest daughter, Emiko (Emmy-Coe), was almost three years old. During that time, I had the pleasure of taking four weeks of paid leave from my corporate job for some daddy-daughter bonding with Reiko while my wife, Mari, went back to work, and while Emiko went to school. During one of the first few mornings I was on leave, Mari was especially flustered prior to heading into work. She had to pump breast milk for Reiko's bottles; she was getting dressed and ready for a day at the office, and she was trying to wrangle Emiko to get the girl's hair done for school. While I was getting dressed, I could tell Mari was getting extremely frustrated by how the morning was going, and she knew she would be late for her first appointment.

That's when I stepped in and said, "Just go to work, I'll take care of Emiko's hair."

Mari chuckled and quipped, "C'mon, you know Reiko doesn't like to be put down alone in the morning. She's going to raise hell while you're getting Emiko's hair done. I'll do it."

After some back and forth, I finally convinced her that I'd take care of it, and she left me with one final parting shot prior to closing the front door: "I'll believe it when I see it."

At that point, I put Reiko in the Ergobaby carrier, placed Emiko on a stool in our bathroom, and I started the process of putting her hair in a ponytail. Easy as pie.

Then I realized my wife was probably at work thinking I would buckle under the pressure and send Emiko to school looking like a female version of Andy Samberg. I needed proof that I had everything under control. Within minutes, I found my camera, placed it on a ten-second timer, and took a quick photo of the scene. Shortly thereafter, Emiko's hair looked great, Reiko was calm, and I sent the photo to Mari with a caption that simply read, "BOOM." We both enjoyed a great laugh from it all, and I figured that would be the end of it.

After dropping Emiko off at school, I put Reiko down for her morning nap and thought my followers would get a kick out of the photo, so I posted it on the Daddy Doin' Work social media pages.

Little did I know what would happen next.

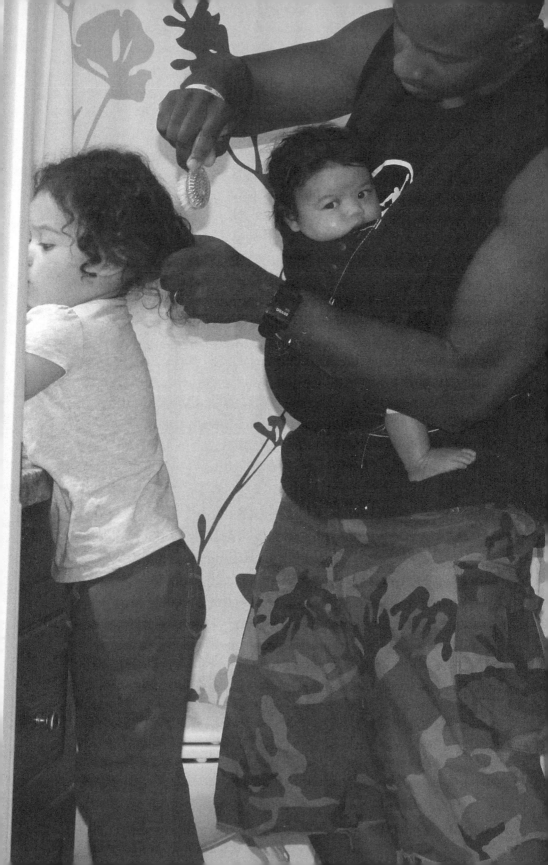

GOING VIRAL—PART I

After making breakfast, I came back to my computer and noticed that the photo was receiving an insane amount of attention, and based on my unscientific analysis, the reactions usually fell into one of three categories: approximately fifteen percent were racists who offered their enlightened opinions on what they thought of black fathers and people who marry outside of their race, or individuals who commented on unrelated items, such as the crappy baby brush I was using or the shower curtain in the background. Twenty five percent were pissed off parents who thought I was trying to get attention for doing things that every good dad should be doing; and about sixty percent were people who thought I was a hero for setting an example for what a good dad should be like.

To nobody's surprise, other social media groups used the photo without crediting me in an attempt to gain more followers for their own brand, which ultimately resulted in me removing the photo from my social media pages after a week or so (not that removing the photo made a bit of difference in that regard).

I would be lying to you if I said the initial reactions didn't affect me. In my time as a blogger, I've posted hundreds of photos of me with my kids, many of which I believe to be much cuter than the one I posted that day; but none of them even received a fraction of the attention this one did. I simply couldn't wrap my head around all of the craziness.

In a quiet moment a few nights later, I wrote a blog post entitled, "I Have A Dream" that outlined what I hoped for the future. The post was a measured counterpunch directed at the racists, insecure dads, and other clowns who took swings at me. But most importantly, it laid out my dream of hoping that a photo of a man taking care of his children wouldn't be viewed as such a monumental occasion. The essay was well received; everyone finally seemed to be on the same page, and at that point I figured that would be the end of it.

I was wrong.

GOING VIRAL—PART II

Two months later, I had enjoyed a small vacation with the family, and the last thing I felt like doing was composing another blog post to run that week. I was burnt out, completely exhausted, and I was busy writing the book you're reading right now. So I figured, "Why not do a 'Best of Daddy Doin' Work' series where I post my best stuff of the year?" That would allow me to spend time with my family and share my most popular work with people who might have missed it. What a brilliant idea! That was when I reposted the photo with the accompanying "I Have A Dream" blog post as the most memorable Daddy Doin' Work moment of the year. Since I included the blog post with the photo that time around, everyone knew the backstory, and it only took a day or two for everyone to offer their opinions and move on to the next shiny object on their newsfeeds.

This would finally be the end of it for sure, right?

Wrong again.

Less than a week after the reposting, an extremely popular website called The Good Men Project ran my photo and blog post, and that was when the Internet broke. In other words, it made what I had experienced a few months prior seem like a bedtime story by comparison. *The Today Show* wanted to interview me, *Good Morning America* wanted to interview me, Katie Couric wanted to interview me, Yahoo! wanted to interview me, *CNN Headline News* wanted to interview me, *The Huffington Post* wanted to interview me, *Sunrise Australia* wanted to interview me, *Mail Online* in the UK wanted to interview me—pretty much every major news outlet wanted a piece of me. While this was going on, my website averaged over 125,000 unique visitors a day, I received thousands of emails (many of which I still haven't read), A-list celebrities re-tweeted my photo, and there was a short period of time when my story became one of the top news stories in the entire world. I couldn't turn on the television or go online without seeing my picture and blog post being talked about somewhere. It was just sheer and utter insanity.

THE INTERNAL CONFLICT

It was a pretty epic experience to fly across the country, meet celebrities, and be interviewed by some of the most respected personalities in the media; however, something just didn't sit well with me about all of this. Why did the photo create a worldwide stir in the first place? Was it because I'm a black guy displaying my skills as a dad? Was it because of the racist and hateful comments I received? Was it because some women thought it looked hot to see an athletic dude in cut-off camouflage shorts and a tank top caring for two little girls? Was it because people were outraged that a random blogger became a worldwide media darling for doing what he's supposed to do as a dad?

Hell, if I know. Probably all of the above, I guess. It was unsettling to see the story become something other than an avenue to open up a dialogue about evolving fatherhood. Most of my close friends and longtime followers know I'll talk about evolving fatherhood until I'm blue in the face, because it's what I'm passionate about. And no, it's not easy for me to turn blue in the face.

Instead, people wanted to talk about how I'm "Super Dad," "The World's Greatest Dad," or "Cliff Huxtable version 2.0." Other men wanted to get in the action by posting photos of themselves wearing babies or brushing their kids' hair as if to say, "Hey, look at me, everybody! I'm a great dad, too!" (As if a cute photo with kids makes anyone a great parent) Some women were pissed because they do these things every day, and nobody even gives them a passing glance. It was just a complete mess . . . a mess that I feel somewhat responsible for creating. Fortunately, I brought my proverbial mop and broom to clean it up once and for all.

If I learned anything from that crazy media tour, it's that the world's perception of what modern fatherhood is all about is completely distorted. Yes, we have made significant strides from thirty or forty years ago in that regard, but by no means is our work done. Many dads (regardless of their racial or ethnic background) are sensitive, nurturing, loving, and affectionate toward their children. Every day more dads are giving up their careers to stay at home with their young children while their spouses work. Dads all over America are brushing and styling their daughters' hair or strapping their babies to their chests proudly. So, why is it that when the aforementioned happens the world goes nuts? Shouldn't these behaviors be expected of modern dads and embraced by everyone else?

If a woman named Betsy Sue Burroughs in Baton Rouge, Louisiana, were to share a similar photo that I posted, do you think it would've broken the Internet? No way. What message does it send to the great dads of the world when a guy can post a photo, and he's looked at as if he's a king? What message does it send to men who think they can take ten seconds out of their lives to take a photo with their kids in hopes of becoming the next viral sensation?

THE ROAD AHEAD

All is not lost. We can fix this.

The first step in dealing with any problem is realizing that we have one. It's essential that men and women understand what is expected of a modern dad, discard any antiquated gender roles, and focus on making the world a better place for our children. If anything, my experience showed me that there's a need for this more than ever, and there's no time like the present to get the ball rolling.

CHAPTER 2

THE GPS TO EVOLVING FATHERHOOD

WHO DO WE ASK FOR help when we don't know which way to go?

The Map! Right. Let's check my backpack, and . . .

Sorry about that. I've watched way too many *Dora The Explorer* episodes lately. By the way, who uses maps anymore? Memo to Dora's parents: if you're going to let your kid roam the countryside unsupervised with a motley crew of talking animals, you should at least invest in a GPS to give her a decent chance of getting home safely. Check that—I wouldn't let my kids run around the countryside unsupervised with a bunch of talking animals in the first place. But hey, I'm not here to judge.

To introduce myself, I'm Doyin (doe-ween) and I'm your faithful tour guide on this trip. As you know, a good tour guide needs a map—err . . . GPS—to show the way. In doing so, let's answer some simple questions, namely, what, who, and how.

THE FINISH LINE (THE WHAT)

My end goal is an extremely ambitious one: to evolve fatherhood across the globe.

So, what exactly does that even mean?

To ensure that all fathers are actively and willingly involved in their kids' lives, emotionally and spiritually, while also being fully engaged parenting partners with their spouses. (That last part isn't applicable to single dads, obviously.)

It means that dads will spend more time reading books to their children at night than ignoring them while surfing the Internet or watching television.

It means dads who work full-time outside of the home will realize that being a dad means more than just bringing home a paycheck and playing the occasional game of catch in the backyard with their kids.

It means dads will always be fifty-fifty parenting partners with their spouses no matter what they have going on in life (unless their spouses are crazy, lazy, or deadbeats, then all bets are off).

It means dads will view the role as the primary male role model in their kids' lives as their most important role.

So yes, it's an extremely ambitious goal, but one that can absolutely be reached.

THE TARGETS (THE WHO)

We've established that we're trying to evolve fatherhood across the globe, so it's pretty obvious that dads are the main targets for this book, right? Well, not exactly.

The last thing most men are interested in is hearing advice from another man on . . . well, anything. Especially if the advice is centered around how well (or not well) they are raising their kids. I'm fine with that. So, here we are in the second chapter of the book, and you're probably wondering, "What does he mean by empowering women to evolve fatherhood?" Great question.

I believe there is a way to evolve fatherhood indirectly, and that's by enlisting women to help. Ladies, nobody knows your men better than you. Hell, in some cases, you know them better than they know themselves. What you'll find in the pages to follow is a backstage pass into the life of dads, and when you're done, you'll know exactly what makes dads tick—and you'll learn ways to make them tick in a way that will lead to happier, healthier relationships with you and your kids. Additionally, you'll take an honest look at yourself to determine if you're part of the solution or part of the problem when it comes to achieving our goals.

Hey fellas, don't roll your eyes at me. Just because this book is geared toward women, it doesn't mean that you won't find it interesting. As a matter of fact, if you're a great dad, you'll love what you're about to read, because it validates everything about how you approach your role as a father.

WHEN BEING SELFISH IS NOT SELFISH (THE WHY)

You could be a longtime follower of my Daddy Doin' Work blog.

You could be a woman stuck with a lazy man who takes zero interest in being a dad, and you want some pointers on how to deal with him.

You could be a woman who has a husband who thinks that all you do as a stay-at-home mom is watch crappy television while he has a "real job," and you're looking for a way to prove to him that you do more work than he could ever imagine.

You could be a woman married to an amazing dad, and you want to ensure he stays that way.

You could be an amazing dad who wants to join the army to evolve fatherhood.

Only you know what motivates you to be here, and since I'm not a mind reader, I'm just going to assume your reason is a good one.

That said, I think it's only fair to let you in on why I wrote this book.

Anyone who knows me knows that I'm a straight shooter, and I promise not to feed you any bullshit as we embark on this journey. So, I'll be honest by saying my goals in writing this book are completely self-serving. No, it has nothing to do with becoming rich or famous; but it has everything to do with my two daughters. Let me explain.

My little girls closed escrow on the center of my universe the moment I laid eyes on them. My oldest daughter, Emiko, is three and a half years old, and she's a Spider-Man impersonating, Nick Jr. obsessed, dimpled chatterbox. My youngest daughter, Reiko, is one year old, and she's a happy, chubby, breastfed baby. Sure, I don't have to worry about either of them getting married or having children anytime soon, but the thought of it scares the hell out of me.

In my time blogging, I often read horror stories from my female readers about deadbeat dads, emotionally-unavailable dads, lazy dads, abusive dads, and the like. As much as I tried, the sheer volume of these stories made it impossible to write them off as isolated incidents. There was a pattern. There was a problem.

The women in these relationships aren't morons. Very few ladies are dumb enough to know ahead of time that a dude isn't suitable to marry or have kids with, still does so anyway, and scratches her head wondering why things in her life are so shitty. The bottom line is, they got *duped*. Everyone in life has been duped before, including you. Hopefully, the ramifications of said duping didn't lead you to raising children with a chump instead of a champ, but if it did, you're not alone.

I'm raising my girls to be careful, street smart, and always have their bullshit-detector switched to the ON position. But what if the one big mistake they make in life has to do with choosing the father of their children? I couldn't live with myself.

To give them the best chance for success, I want to use this book to ensure more current and future dads become—or continue to be—the awesome dads their families deserve.

Fortunately, my selfish goal of doing whatever it takes to make this goal a reality for the sake of my children benefits your children as well. It ensures your sons grow up to be hard-working, loving, chivalrous men who put the needs of their family before anything else. It ensures your daughters won't have to kiss a ridiculous amount of nasty frogs (and I hate frogs, by the way) in order to find a prince who will cherish her and their children. It's totally doable, but I'll need an army to defeat formidable enemies we're up against.

MOM UP (THE HOW)

If you're a mom in a relationship with a lazy, couch-surfing man who refuses to take part in raising your children, that's completely okay. Well, it's *not* okay, but it's okay if you're willing to own it and not make weak excuses for why you're in the situation you're in. Be warned, you will read a lot of tough love in the following pages. None of it is meant to make you feel like a failure as a person or a mom, but it's meant to serve as a wake up call to make the requisite changes in order to lead a healthy and happy life. We're going to dissect the three types of dads (yes, there are only three of them), and by the time you finish this book, you'll know what motivates them and how to handle them. Just know that it will require you to have a thick skin and not take anything personally.

Are you willing to be open minded? Are you willing to make life-altering paradigm shifts? Good. Keep reading.

Overall, this book will have a conversational tone to it. Just picture me and you enjoying a nice, relaxed talk without any barriers. No, our children won't be around for this conversation, and because of that, there's a chance you'll come across some colorful language every now and then. I'm assuming you're not the type to be offended by the occasional curse word, but hey, if you can deal with everything parenthood throws at you without uttering a swear word or two, you're a better person than me.

And finally, you'll find a lot of stories included that come directly from the Daddy Doin' Work Facebook page and emails from my Subscribers Doin' Work (otherwise known as my email subscribers). These are real stories from real parents with real issues, and with the exception of Chapter 20, I changed the names of my readers and their family members to protect their privacy.

Now that you know our objectives, I bet you have some questions for me.

Are you trying to appease yourself to women by bashing men?

Nope. I'm going to be really tough on the women reading this. So much so that some of them will be upset with me by the time they make it to the end of the book. I'm not in the business of sugar coating anything because that won't lead to real progress. If moms are playing a role in why the men in their lives aren't doing their jobs effectively as dads and husbands, they're going to hear about it. Bluntly. No punches will be pulled.

On the other hand, men who are loving, caring, and involved dads and husbands will be celebrated here. They are the gold standard that all men should strive for. Why would I want to alienate them? We're on the same team. I'll always celebrate these great men.

Crappy dads? Well, they'll be bashed here. But you probably knew that was coming. The same goes for the dads who think they're rock stars just because they bring home a paycheck while simultaneously complaining that their stay-at-home wives or girlfriends do nothing but "sit on their asses all day." But it's more than bashing these men. It's about empowering women in relationships with them to be the catalyst for change or get the hell out.

There are shitty moms out there, too, you know. Why aren't you talking about them?

The short answer is, because this is a book about fatherhood, not motherhood.

The longer answer is yes, that's correct. There are many horrible moms out there wreaking havoc on families across the world. However, I think we can agree that they're on the fringe. In other words, how often do you see these women? Can you honestly say you see just as many crappy moms as you do crappy dads? I doubt it.

There's a reason for that. Between the exhaustion of diaper changing, late-night breastfeeding, driving the kids to soccer practice, and helping with homework, most (but certainly not all) moms view motherhood as being a cool gig. Being a good mom is a badge of honor that women strive for daily.

Obviously, there are men who also view fatherhood as cool (including yours truly), but there's a population of dads who thinks getting married and having kids is just part of the plan, and feels no passion about the job. For some, it's not even about lacking passion for the job—they just flat out despise the tasks of fatherhood.

Fatherhood is damn cool. As a matter of fact, it's the coolest thing a man can ever do. The goal is to evolve fatherhood to the point where it will be extremely difficult to find a man who doesn't take extreme pride in being a good dad.

Who died and made you the expert on parenting?

Unfortunately, people die everyday, but in the history of the universe, a parenting expert never died because none ever existed. We talked about this already. I'm not a parenting expert; however, I do know what it takes to be a good dad. I also intimately understand the pain women endure with slowly-evolved dads and deadbeat dads, because I've corresponded with thousands of moms about this topic for years.

I'm not a doctor, a psychologist, or family counselor—and trust me, that's a good thing. I'm not going to throw out five-dollar words to show you how smart I am, I'm not going to bore you to tears by filling this book with empirical data, and I'm not going to lecture you as if you're a naughty child. I'm your friend, your homie, your confidante, who will offer tough love if needed; I'm your dad-on-the-street-who-knows-his-shit.

I'm here to share my personal experiences and those of my readers in order for you to enjoy a fresh and modern look into the world of fatherhood.

Do you think you can really put an end to the crappy dad dilemma? That's a tall order, sir.

Right. But can we first agree that there are many more good dads in this world than crappy ones? Actually, it really isn't very close.

However, it's true. It absolutely is a tall order to deal with the small pocket of fathers giving the rest of us a bad name by negatively impacting their spouses and children. I'm sure the critics of the Wright brothers (and probably the Wright brothers themselves) thought it was a tall order to make heavy machinery move through the sky like a bird, but the brothers did it anyway.

If this task was as simple as a walk in the park, it would be done by now. The reason why it's not done is because this isn't a job that can be achieved by any one person. I'm driving the tour bus, but I still need passengers. A lot of them. Once we have enough people on the bus saying, "Enough is enough, and we're not going to put up with this anymore," is when real progress will be made. This book is intended to be the starting point.

Hopefully, I answered your questions effectively. If not, don't fret, because there's a good chance I'll cover what's on your mind as we dive in. Now, let's transition by meeting the players in the game of fatherhood.

CHAPTER 3

THE DIVISION OF DADDIES

DARKNESS INTO LIGHT

I remember the rainy December night vividly. Our unborn baby was dead.

Yes, I knew that complications could occur in the first trimester, but not to *us*. Everything in our lives was good and easy up to that point; so why would that be any different? Make love with wife. Wife gets pregnant. Happy, healthy baby appears nine months later. It was a very simple and straightforward plan of action to follow . . . or so I thought.

While I grieved the loss of our unborn baby, it gave me an opportunity to reflect on my motivation to become a father in the first place. Did I want it simply because every other dude around me was married with kids? Or was it deeper than that? It didn't take long for me to realize I'd give up anything to raise a child. That was all I wanted. While alone with my thoughts, I promised myself that if we were lucky enough to have a baby, I would be the best dad I could ever be for him or her. All I wanted was *a chance*.

After what seemed like the longest wait ever, I finally became a father to my beautiful daughter Emiko two years later, and nothing could have prepared me for what happened from that point on.

When I held her for the first time, I felt a rush of emotion I will never forget for as long as I'm alive. I cried, laughed, and felt as if I could leap tall buildings with a single bound. As I wheeled her bassinet down the empty hospital hallway to witness her first bath, I whispered to her, "Hi, Emiko. I'm not perfect, but I will dedicate my life to ensuring yours is as amazing as possible. I love you, kiddo." She was sleeping peacefully, but I know she heard me.

As any new parent can attest to, the first few weeks were an absolute blur. Between the lack of sleep and doing everything I could to ensure my kid survived each day, I never really took any time to assess how I was doing the job. Sure, I wanted to be a dad, but was I doing the job *well?*

Through a stroke of randomness, I had a conversation with a stranger when my daughter was three months old, and it changed how I viewed myself as a father.

To set the stage, one of Mari's best friends was getting married and we were able to bring Emiko with us to the ceremony and reception. Since my wife was a bridesmaid and couldn't spend much time with the baby, I told her to have fun with her girlfriends and I'd enjoy a daddy-daughter night with my baby girl. During the course of the evening, I fed her bottles, changed her poopy diapers, danced with her, calmed her from multiple meltdowns, and held her while she slept. Just another day as a dad as far as I was concerned.

I mean, there isn't a dad on the planet that wouldn't do this for his child and his wife, right?

As the night ended, a young lady approached me, and we had the following conversation:

Young lady: "I gotta say, I watched you with your baby all night. I can just see the love on your face. It's heart-warming to witness."

Me: "Thank you so much, but I'm only doing what comes naturally to me."

Young lady: "You'd be surprised by the amount of fathers who would not do what you did tonight. The world needs to see more dads like you."

On the drive home from the wedding, I thought about how I promised to be the best dad possible when I mourned the loss of my unborn child a couple of years prior. Is it true that caring for my daughter—something that comes as naturally to me as breathing—is something many men wouldn't do for their kids? Quite honestly, I thought I was going to have an aneurysm trying to figure out how some dads cannot or will not step up for the most important job of their lives.

Now that I have three and a half years of daddy experience under my belt, I have many more answers as to why some fathers are the way they are. Through observations and interviews with men and women of all ages and ethnicities, I've learned that every dad falls into one of three categories. Yes, I'm throwing a blanket over every single man who fathered a baby, and there are absolutely no exceptions to this scientific rule.

The dads in each category present their own unique challenges for today's families, and we will cover them all in detail.

But first, let's introduce the players.

DADDIES DOIN' NOTHING

Remember when you were in high school or college and you had to complete a group assignment with someone? You and your partner divided up the tasks evenly and agreed to your roles, responsibilities, and timelines. You would check in with your partner weekly to ensure everything was on track, and each time he would provide you with a lame excuse as to why he couldn't provide his deliverable to you.

"Hey, I've been sick this week—but don't worry, I'll have my assignment ready for the next meeting."

Or

"I have all of my notes at home, but I'm totally on top of everything. Relax."

This wasn't some rinky dink assignment; it was worth *fifty percent of your total grade* for the course, so you believed he would take this as seriously as you did.

A week before the assignment was due you held your final meeting to review progress. Yep, you guessed it; the dude brought nothing with him except for more lame excuses and broken promises. You stayed up late, you sacrificed time with your friends and family to get the necessary work done, and you believed your partner when he said he would do his part.

In retrospect, there were clear signs indicating he wouldn't step up, but you chose to ignore them and it resulted in one hundred percent of the responsibility falling on your weary shoulders. After spending time feeling sorry for yourself and questioning your intelligence for face-planting into this guy's steaming pile of bullshit, you pulled yourself together because that project *needed* to be completed no matter what.

The good news is, you were strong enough to pick up the

pieces and submit a stellar project, even though it ended up being much harder than it needed to be.

The bad news is your partner unapologetically took credit for *your* work and received the same "A" grade as you for doing absolutely nothing.

In the world of fatherhood, these are the characteristics of a Daddy Doin' Nothing.

We all have experience with these men. We've worked with them, went to school with them, and some of you even dated them. You'll find them from Brooklyn to Beverly Hills, and they come in all shapes, sizes, ages, and colors. My hope is that you weren't raised by one, or had any kids with one, because once children are involved, the stakes and difficulty increase exponentially.

These guys are lazy, selfish, manipulative, and sneaky—but they aren't stupid. They know *exactly* what they're doing and often play to the insecurities of their partners to get what they want.

A Daddy Doin' Nothing refuses to look for work because he knows his wife has a good enough job to pay the bills.

A Daddy Doin' Nothing plops his kid in front of a TV screen for hours on end without interacting with her and calls it parenting.

A Daddy Doin' Nothing uses Popeye the Sailor Man's "I am what I am" philosophy to make excuses for his shitty behavior.

A Daddy Doin' Nothing talks a big game, but when the chips are down, one hundred percent of the parenting responsibilities fall on the shoulders of his wife, girlfriend, or baby mama.

A Daddy Doin' Nothing loves to verbally and physically abuse his wife and kids because he's too much of a punk to demonstrate his version of "toughness" on someone his own size.

Don't fret, because just like the High School project we described earlier, hope is not lost. If you're involved with a Daddy Doin' Nothing, I'm not going to insult your intelligence by simply stating, "Do whatever you can to work it out." Quite frankly, in many cases, your relationship will not (and should not) survive, and that's a good thing. The main priority is doing whatever it takes to protect your children from a crappy male role model.

In the chapters to follow, we'll examine all of the under-handed tricks these dads use to their advantage, and how to beat them. We'll also differentiate between a Daddy Doin' Nothing and a traditional deadbeat dad. Most importantly, we will review the steps women must take to personally evolve and ensure they never involve themselves with these toxic men now or ever again.

Ladies, never let a Daddy Doin' Nothing drag you down on your parenting project. Either you're going to divide the work equally to get an "A" or you're going to expose him to the world for being the fraud he is and *still* get that "A" by yourself or with an active partner.

DADDIES DOIN' SOMETHING

Remember the iconic cartoon *The Flintstones?* Growing up I think I watched every episode, but my favorite of all time went like this:

Fred had a particularly stressful day busting rocks at the quarry, and his boss, Mr. Slate, was riding him like Secretariat from the moment he arrived in the morning until the moment he left in the evening. The poor guy forgot his lunch at home, suffered from a horrible headache, and was completely exhausted.

Once he got home, Fred acted as if everything that happened during the course of his day was a distant memory. He hugged and kissed his stay-at-home wife Wilma, he sat his toddler daughter, Pebbles, on his lap and read stories to her, and he even offered to cook dinner for the family so Wilma could take a much-needed break from her monotonous domestic duties.

Man, I loved that episode.

The problem is, that episode *never happened*.

Don't get me wrong here; even though Fred is a loud, animated, and borderline obnoxious dude, he's also a good guy with a good heart. Nobody would question how much he loves Wilma and Pebbles, but unfortunately there is no chance he would act as I described in that fake episode. After a typical day at the quarry, he would open the door and yell, "Wilma! I'm home! What's for dinner? I'm starving!" Afterwards, he'd plop down on his rock couch and crack open a cold Cactus Cola, because that's what dads in the stone ages did after work.

Wilma's role was to handle everything in the home. She didn't seem to mind, because . . . well, that's what moms of the stone ages were expected to do. From my childhood assessment, she wasn't educated and didn't really care to be. Taking care of the household duties, raising Pebbles, and keeping Fred happy were the only things that really mattered to her.

Luckily we're not in the stone ages anymore, and mothers have evolved at a remarkably rapid rate over the years. Many are college educated, hold prestigious titles in the corporate workplace, and pride themselves on never needing to depend on a man for anything. Additionally, if mothers stay at home with their children, it is because they *choose* to do so, not because they lack the requisite skills or education to find a good career.

Fathers, too, have evolved since the caveman days, but the pace is oftentimes painstakingly slow. Even today I bet you know a man who kicks off his shoes, turns on the TV, and doesn't do a damn thing around the house or with the kids. Hell, he could be *your* man. Why does this happen? Because similar to Fred Flintstone, these dads believe their main responsibility is to bring home money to the family. They'll bring home the bacon, but don't you dare ask them to cook it.

Of the three types of dads, these men pose a unique problem because they're not deadbeats, but they're not going to win any Father of the Year awards either. Simply stated, on a scale of 1–10, they would be holding steady in the 4–6 range, which equates to "good enough." And just like their title says, at least they are Daddies Doin' *Something*.

Should we give them credit for the hard work put in at work and cut them some slack when they're with their families? Or should we push them to become active and engaged partners and parents no matter how exhausting and stressful the workday is? We all know the right answer.

And by the way, here's a newsflash to everyone reading this: when we have children, we are going to be exhausted. It doesn't matter if it is a stay-at-home parent or the vice president of a Fortune 500 company; kids have a way of sapping the energy out of us. With that said, dads who work outside of the home have the option to act like Fred Flintstone because they have no energy left to give, or they can push through the fatigue and be the dads their kids deserve. Unfortunately, the men in this category choose the first option far too often, and that creates unnecessary stress on the family unit.

The bottom line here is that the Daddies Doin' Something need to evolve *quickly*. Gone are the days when they can say they're great dads because they hold a steady job and take their kids to the park once a month. Modern mothers are a hell of a lot more evolved on average than Wilma Flintstone; however, in many cases the wardrobe is the only differentiator between a Daddy Doin' Something and Wilma's loud-mouthed, cave-man husband. As a dad to two little girls, I'd be heartbroken if they married men who expected them to do all of the cooking, cleaning, and child raising. We have to demand better from these men for the sake of our kids and our grandkids.

With that goal in mind, in future chapters we will review exactly how these men can quickly evolve, and it starts by teaching them how to think with a mom's mindset. And no, thinking with a mom's mindset doesn't mean that dads will forfeit the ownership of their testicles in the process.

DADDIES DOIN' WORK

These dads get it. No matter how busy their days are, they are enthusiastically involved whenever they are around their children. Doin' Work to them means stepping up by comforting a crying infant in the middle of the night, playing dress up with their daughters, teaching their sons how to be gentlemen, and stepping up for their exhausted spouses without being asked to do so. They can be corporate hotshots or stay-at-home dads, but the common theme with these men is that nothing is more important than ensuring their families are happy and loved. In other words, the main difference between a Daddy Doin' Work and the other types of dads is that they always put the needs of their families before their own. Are these dads perfect? Of course not, but any reasonable person could observe them and instantly determine that they take the job of being an involved father very seriously.

In the coming chapters, you will become acquainted with the various types of these great men, and we'll learn more about their unique challenges as they navigate through fatherhood. Some of those challenges are created by society, some are self-inflicted, and some are created by the women they partner with. Either way, it will be covered in detail.

What category does your man fall into?

SECTION 1
DADDIES DOIN' NOTHING

CHAPTER 4

DEADBEAT DADS 2.0

A TRAGIC LOVE STORY

Let me tell you a story about Matthew and Lisa.

Lisa is a young lady living in Los Angeles and working as a project manager for a large insurance company. She loves her job and is very good at it, but something in her life was missing. As a woman in her late twenties, she desperately wanted to find love and start a family of her own. In the past eighteen months, she was invited to four different weddings, and she felt it was time to step her game up, stop working late at the office, and enter the dating scene.

While at a large birthday for one of her friends, she met a really nice man named Matthew. He worked in construction, was really charming, had a killer smile, was very athletic, and he knew exactly what to say to keep Lisa interested. After the party ended, they spent hours talking at a nearby park about everything ranging from politics to music to sports. The connection she felt with him was unlike anything she'd experienced before, and she was excited for what the future had in store for them.

After eight months of dating, Matthew moved in with Lisa,

and a few weeks later, she found out that she was pregnant with his baby. At first, she was worried about telling him for fear that he would be scared off, but he mentioned in the past how much he enjoys children, so her trepidation dissipated quickly.

When Lisa finally told Matthew about the news, he seemed excited. He loved Lisa and said that he couldn't wait to be a dad, but unfortunately his words and actions were not aligned. As the months progressed during Lisa's pregnancy, she noticed that Matthew became distant. He didn't help with meals, he didn't clean the house, he didn't participate in decorating their son's room, and he spent a lot of time after work at the gym or the sports bar. Lisa didn't make anything of it, and just figured that her fear was due to her pregnancy hormones raging.

When their son Jake was born, Matthew didn't shed any tears of joy and he didn't smile. He wouldn't even hold the baby because he didn't want to "drop him on the floor by accident." Again, Lisa just assumed that he was just overwhelmed by the enormity of the moment and didn't make a big deal of it.

Two and a half months into Jake's life, Matthew's latest construction contract ran out and he was out of a job. This happened before and he always found other work, so Lisa wasn't too worried. But then she had an idea. Since she brought home a six-figure salary as project manager, she suggested that she could work while he stayed at home with the baby. Matthew agreed and the problem was solved. Her maternity leave was ending in two weeks, so she was relieved to know that her son would be at home with his father instead of at daycare.

Unfortunately, the problems began once Lisa returned to work. After a week back on the job, she came home one day to find the baby lying in his crib in an extremely dirty diaper while Matthew was watching television. She couldn't believe what she was seeing. Confused and angry, Lisa demanded to know what was going on. Without diverting his attention from the sports highlight show he was watching, he rolled his eyes and snapped, "Look, he's not crying. I was just about to change him. Get off my back." After waiting for about ten seconds to see if he would budge from the couch, she picked up Jake and changed him herself. Since this was the first time this happened, she just figured that maybe he had had a bad day. Or maybe he was upset about the fact that he was not working in construction anymore. After mulling it over, she felt he deserved a break and apologized for being so harsh on him.

Weeks passed and the same behavior continued. Whenever Lisa came home from work, Jake would have a rotten diaper attached to his rear end, the apartment would be a complete mess, dinner wouldn't be made, and Matthew would be plopped in front of the television like a beached whale. Additionally, he refused to wake up in the middle of the night to change diapers or feed bottles to the baby. His excuse was he needed "extra energy to keep up with Jake" during the day, and anything less than eight hours of uninterrupted sleep wasn't going to cut it. "Keep up with Jake?" It's not like he was a toddler creating havoc—he was just a baby that couldn't even crawl yet. Regardless, Lisa didn't question him and woke up every night to care for the baby even though she had to work for ten hours at the office every Monday through Friday.

One day, Lisa received a phone call at work from Matthew's mother, Karen (a retired nurse living ten miles away from their apartment), wondering where he was. Baffled by her question, Lisa assumed that he was home with the baby. Treading lightly, Karen asked if Lisa knew about the arrangement Matthew made with her. Before Lisa could answer, she could hear

Jake crying in the background. The whole time Lisa thought Matthew was watching Jake, he'd actually dropped the baby off at his mother's house while he stayed home alone. She was pissed.

Fuming, Lisa canceled her meetings for the day and drove home to find Matthew on the couch asleep. She was ready to throw him out, but he came up with an elaborate story of how he was depressed from losing his job and he really wanted to be a good dad—he left the baby with his mother just so the baby wouldn't be exposed to his moods. After agreeing to visit a therapist, Lisa gave him a second chance.

After months of half-assing therapy (meaning, showing up whenever he felt like it), nothing changed. He would still drop Jake off at his mother's house occasionally, and on the days he spent at home with him, Jake would be found dirty and hungry whenever Lisa walked through the front door. Every day it was a different excuse for why it happened, and every day Lisa bought it. She wasn't happy with her relationship, but she didn't want to start over again. At least Jake had a dad. A lot of kids aren't lucky enough to be raised in a two-parent household, so she viewed that as a positive. Overall, Jake didn't seem to be unhappy either, so that helped Lisa to feel better about the situation as well. She knew having children wouldn't be easy, so she was ready to just grin and bear it. That's what any good parent would do, right?

BREAKDOWN

The story of Matthew and Lisa is real, and they stayed together until Jake was two years old when she finally called it quits.

We'll get to Lisa's role in this a little bit later, but if you could use one word to describe Matthew, what would it be? I'm sure a lot of the words you came up with aren't very flattering, but would you use the word "deadbeat?" Depending on whom you ask, some will say that a deadbeat is defined only as someone who leaves the family and refuses to financially support his children.

That may be true, but in my mind, being a deadbeat encompasses much more than being a yellow-bellied sperm donor who skips town because he isn't man enough to raise his own kids. It's more than forgetting his kids' birthdays or not being *physically* present in his kids' lives. As a matter of fact, that form of a deadbeat dad won't even be addressed in this book. That's not to say that these guys don't cause heartache and strife in households all over the world, because they do; but the bottom line is they *aren't there*.

The deadbeat dads I choose to focus on are a lot scarier than the losers you couldn't find without the assistance of a search party. Deadbeat Dads 2.0, also known as Daddies Doin' Nothing, don't help out their families financially, but instead of skipping town, they live under the same roof as their spouses and children, making the lives of everyone involved extremely difficult. They break promises to their kids repeatedly, they lie to their spouses constantly, and they spend more time parked on the couch or drinking at the bar than they do interacting with their families.

It would seem logical that the psychological damage a kid can endure by having an emotionally unavailable dad at home is way worse than not having him around at all. Everyone needs love and guidance, but who needs it more than children? At least when a traditional deadbeat dad isn't around, kids will receive love from their mothers. When a Daddy Doin' Nothing is in the picture, kids will expect the same love from him that they receive from their moms, and they'll come up empty every time.

This is a problem—a huge problem—but every problem has a solution, and this is no exception.

CHAPTER 5
FACES OF THE ENEMY

THEY ARE EVERYWHERE

Daddies Doin' Nothing are everywhere. They can be young or old, white or black, rich or poor, famous celebrities, or Joe/Jane Every-Person.

Yes, we all know women can be shitty parents, too; but since this is a book about evolving fatherhood, we're going to put the crosshairs squarely on the men who offer zero tangible (and intangible) value to their families. Like wrecking balls, Daddies Doin' Nothing are destroying families everywhere, and their spouses and children are left to pick up the pieces.

Ladies, if you're unfortunate enough to be involved with a Daddy Doin' Nothing, do you remember what it was like when you first met him? Chances are he wasn't wearing a sign around his neck that read, "WARNING! I'M A LOSER AND A DEADBEAT! PROCEED WITH CAUTION!" Instead, he was handsome, charming, charismatic, and funny. It didn't take too long for you to determine he was the guy you wanted to spend your life with and become the father of your children.

Then *it* happened.

It has many forms, but you know *it* when you see it. Everything started to change. He became moody, irritable, distant, lazy, emotionally unavailable, and just plan unpleasant to be around. After a while, you began to question your judgment and sanity for wanting to date or marry a guy like him in the first place. Most importantly, he leaves you on a parenting island to fend for yourself as you attempt to raise your children alone.

He doesn't lift a finger to help with parenting duties, he never gets up in the middle of the night to tend to your crying baby; he will keep his baby in poopy diapers for hours until you come home to change him or her, and he breaks promises to you and your kids repeatedly.

Your days are long, your nights are longer, and you have no idea how you're going to survive another minute without getting some restful sleep. Unfortunately, your man couldn't give a damn about your pain, because he would rather sit on his ass than offer any support to you. A nervous breakdown seems inevitable.

Does any of this sound familiar? Hopefully, not. But if it does, we'll discuss how to handle these men. But first, in order to completely understand how to defeat the enemy, we have to understand the different variations of them.

I-WAS-RAISED-THIS-WAY DADDY DOIN' NOTHING

This guy blames his lack of involvement on his upbringing. Oftentimes his father wasn't around, and if he was around, the last thing he provided was a healthy example of what a dad should be like. His father was abusive, lazy, aloof, or showed zero interest in raising children or being a supportive husband.

If a young man witnesses this behavior from his #1 male role model on a daily basis, it wouldn't be too surprising if he turns out to be just like him. This dynamic is not to be under-estimated. As you read these words, there could be a young, impressionable boy in a household near you watching his father do absolutely nothing to support his wife and children, and thinking that it's okay. Quite frankly, if you're involved with a Daddy Doin' Nothing, that young, impressionable boy could be your son.

Emily, a mom of a three-year-old boy shares her experience:

"My boyfriend does absolutely nothing to help our family financially, emotionally, or spiritually, but I guess I shouldn't be surprised. His dad was lazy, couldn't keep a job, and made life miserable for him and his mother. He kept telling me all of the right things in regards to breaking the cycle, but his actions only demonstrate that he's going to be just like his father. I'll be damned if our son grows up to be like this, but I don't know what to do at this point."

Accountability is not a word that you'll find in the vocabulary of these men.

PEER PRESSURE DADDY DOIN' NOTHING

I remember when I was in high school and college, and I wanted to be popular at all costs. Usually, that entailed behaving like the other "cool kids" while oftentimes being a jerk to those who couldn't reach my level of social influence. Fortunately, I grew out of that phase relatively early in my adulthood. Others aren't so fortunate, and when they become dads, it's even worse.

The Peer Pressure Daddy Doin' Nothing is concerned with

one thing only: appearing to be cool to his male friends. When those friends are Neanderthals who think it's cool to spend countless nights of the week away from their families under the guise of "male bonding," it's not going to end well for his spouse and children.

It's even worse when he's with his friends while also in the presence of his spouse and children. More often than not, he'll hear the following snickers from his buddies.

"Ha! You change diapers? You're such a pussy-whipped little bitch."

"Take your skirt off. It's your woman's job to take care of your crying baby. Sit down and have a beer."

"So, you're really going to sit inside and play with dolls with your kid instead of drinking with us at the bar? You suck, man."

Instead of standing up for himself, he'll do whatever it takes to make his friends happy.

Think about that for a moment. This guy would rather impress a bunch of knuckleheaded dudes than be present for the woman he made vows with and the babies he's supposed to love unconditionally. That makes sense, how exactly?

Louise, a mom to three girls, knows this all too well:

"My husband is always surrounded by his friends and when they're together it's like a fraternity house. Whenever I ask him to help with our daughters, his friends will laugh or roll their eyes at me as if to say that it's not a man's job to do these things. Because of that, he'll snap at me and say he's busy and I should be the one changing diapers, getting them dressed, brushing their

hair, etc. He's more interested in making himself appear to be 'the man' in front of these guys, but he's far from being 'the man' for this family."

Yes, even in this day and age, guys like this exist. Let's keep it real—any man who takes part in this behavior is an embarrassment to real men everywhere. Actually, to call these clowns "men" is a damn insult to any card-carrying member of "Team Grown Ass Man." If a dude values the opinions of his friends more than those of his family, he should never get married or have children to begin with.

DOLLAR BILLS DADDY DOIN' NOTHING

He's driving the newest model European luxury car, he has the fanciest smart phone, and you'll never see him wearing clothes not made by some cat with a name nobody can pronounce. On the surface, he has his shit together, and is the perfect illustration of success.

Not so much.

Dig a little deeper and you'll find out what he's all about. He doesn't have a steady job and makes his money working at "under the table" jobs (I'll let you figure out what that means). His fancy luxury car is parked in the garage of a crappy apartment complex where he lives with his spouse and children, and they barely have enough money to pay the monthly bills.

His kids are practically sleeping on top of each other in a tiny bedroom, they eat cold cereal for each meal, and in the wintertime you'll find his kids shivering at the bus stop without jackets to keep themselves warm. But who cares about those whiny brats? At least he's rolling around town in his car with his heated leather seats and shiny spinning rims. Because, you know, that's what *really* matters.

Here's a story from Rebecca, a mom of two:

> *"I have two children with my boyfriend and he has a Mercedes SUV, a pair of $500 shades, and a closet full of designer clothes. He does contract work, but I don't have a clue what that actually means, because he's very secretive about it. I work full-time as a receptionist for a large telecommunications company, and I don't make a ton of money, but I give almost every dollar I earn to my family. My boyfriend never gives us a dime of his money, but he has no problems driving his fancy car, getting bottle service at the club with his boys, and letting us live in a small apartment in the bad side of town. When I asked him for money to help purchase clothes for the upcoming school year, he said that I should just let them wear the clothes they used last year (which are way too small now). He's the most selfish person I've ever come across and I regret the day I met him."*

If there's a guy I'd like to roundhouse kick into unconsciousness, it would be this fool. I can just picture what people will say about him at his funeral.

"You know what was great about, Johnny? He had the nicest car. Oh, and his clothes, they were always designer. You'd never see him rocking any Wal-Mart gear. What an inspiration. He will be missed."

Bullshit.

Memo to this asshat: When you're dead nobody is going to give a shit about your car or your clothes. Actually, nobody gives a shit about your car or your clothes while you're alive. Grow up out of your "Little Boy Syndrome" and take care of your family.

MIND TERRORIST DADDY DOIN' NOTHING

You can call these dads a lot of things, but you can't call them stupid. Arguably, these men are the worst of the bunch, because they're so manipulative and make women question their sanity on a regular basis. Here are two versions:

Showtime Dads

Here's an obscure reference for you: Remember the old Looney Tunes cartoon that featured Michigan J. Frog? If not, the story is about a man who happened to find a frog that could sing beautifully, and the guy thought he could make millions off of the frog. The problem is that the frog would only sing in front of him, and whenever it was put in front of large crowds, it just did the "ribbit" thing that all frogs do. The guy kept telling everyone who would listen that this frog *could* sing, but people just rolled their eyes as if he were insane. And if I remember correctly, the frog actually drove the dude to insanity.

Showtime Dads are similar, but in the opposite way. More often than not, these guys won't lift a finger around the house unless it's to eat a sandwich or use the remote control. However, when one of his wife's friends stops by the house or there's a family gathering of some kind, the dude transforms into Super Dad. He'll change every diaper, he'll sing songs to his baby, he'll play dress up with his daughter, he'll wash dishes, and overall, he'll be the best guy ever.

Once the guests leave the building, so does his Academy Award winning performance. He's back to playing video games, surfing the net, and ignoring everyone in his family. When his spouse complains to her friends about her husband's lack of family involvement, they'll respond by saying, "Are you kidding? He's amazing! I see how involved he is with your kids and how he helps you around the house. You are SO lucky to have him. Stop complaining . . . you look really selfish and ungrateful right now." It's enough to make these women lose their minds.

Don't be fooled. Showtime Dads know *exactly* what they're doing.

It-Could-Be-Worse Dads

These guys are similar to the Showtime Dads in the sense that they don't lift a finger around the house, but they don't make any effort to put on an act when friends and family stop by either. Instead, once he receives any complaints from his wife, he'll just say,

"You really need to stop whining. At least I . . . (insert one of the following)"

. . . don't beat you up

. . . don't sleep around with other women

. . . don't beat the kids up

. . . am not in jail

. . . am not a crack dealer

Yes, there are some men out there who think you should plan a parade route for them just because they don't beat the crap out of their family members or have sex with random women. And yes, I wouldn't blame you if you felt that the apocalypse is imminent because of it.

Donna is a mom to an infant, and has the unfortunate "pleasure" of being involved with a man who fell into both categories:

> *"My boyfriend is a deadbeat, but nobody knows about it but me. Whenever my family or friends come over, he's the most helpful guy in the world toward our son. He plays with him, changes his diapers, takes him on walks, and even puts him in the baby carrier. My mom thinks he's the best dad on the planet and tells my son that she hopes he grows up to be just like his daddy. Unfortunately, I know the truth. When it's just the three of us alone, he does nothing to help the family financially or emotionally. In many cases, he justifies his behavior by saying at least he's not cheating on me. Is this what it comes down to? I should feel lucky to be in this relationship because he's not sleeping with other women? As sad as it sounds, I'm almost starting to believe that it's true."*

These guys are so convincing with their rhetoric that many women start thinking, "You know? Maybe he has a point. Maybe he's a better dad than I give him credit for." I know that is nonsense, and so do you, but that doesn't change the fact that many women struggle with these men every day.

Believe it or not, this list doesn't include everyone on the Daddy Doin' Nothing team, and the next chapter will introduce you to the people these men depend on to keep their act going. I have a feeling you know who I'm talking about.

CHAPTER 6

LADIES, ARE YOU PART OF THE PROBLEM?

WE'VE IDENTIFIED THE ENEMY. YOU'RE angry. You want to put his testicles in a vice grip until he yells his own name when asked who the biggest punk ass man on the planet is. But hold the phone; unfortunately, in many households around the world these men have allies who keep them relevant.

Women.

Strange, right? These guys wreak their disgusting flavor of havoc and negatively impact families all over the world, and there are women who actually support them at the detriment of themselves and their own children.

Don't get me wrong here; not *all* women, but there are a few out there who are part of the problem, instead of the solution. Ladies, I created this book for you because I truly believe that you hold the key to evolving fatherhood. In the previous chapter, we looked externally, and now we're going to look internally by identifying the telltale signs of an enabler to Daddies Doin' Nothing.

Remember Lisa from earlier? She would be the first to tell you now that she was just as much to blame for her situation as Matthew was, because she allowed the behavior to continue for as long as she did. Luckily, she woke up and got out for the sake of her son and her emotional well-being. But it took her years to do so.

This is a really touchy topic, and it's important to state that no one is on trial here. Based on my observations and interviews with former enablers of these "men," I was able to dissect them into five major categories, and you'll find some real life examples on the following pages. If you're in a relationship with one of these dudes, take a moment to be honest with yourself and determine if you're exhibiting these traits.

1—You make excuses for your man's bad behavior

Imagine if you visited a local park and you noticed a little boy roughhousing and beating the crap out of every kid he came in contact with. After giving his mother the stink eye, you found her glaring back at you, and snapped, "Look, boys will be boys! If your kids can't take it, maybe you shouldn't have them play here!"

Say what? This lady looked at you with a straight face and said it was *your* fault that your kids weren't tough enough to deal with being kicked in the face repeatedly by her obnoxious son. Because, hey, boys will be boys, right? Chances are you'd think this woman is Fifty Shades of Insane and a crappy mother for making excuses for her son's horrible behavior. Nobody would be surprised if this kid grew up to become the high school bully, and if so, his mom would probably say, "If your kid hadn't done X, my son wouldn't have beaten the ever living shit out of him/her."

This is no different when it comes to relationships with Daddies Doin' Nothing. Everyone on the outside can see that these women are involved with deadbeats, but for some reason they make some of the lamest excuses known to mankind to justify why they've put up with them for so long. I've spoken to many women who tell me that this is the number one reason why they stayed in relationships with these men.

If their men are watching television for hours on end and not helping out with the kids, the enablers excuse it by saying they need to unwind.

If their men are out constantly drinking with their friends at the bar, instead of being at home with their families, the enablers excuse it by saying they deserve their male bonding time.

One of my readers, Michelle, dealt with this for a long time:

"I enabled a deadbeat for years. We had a son together and he absolutely refused to help out with him. When I came home from work, he would be home sleeping or surfing the Internet. You know the one thing he wouldn't do? Look for a job. I told him that I'd be fine with him being a stay-at-home dad, but he wasn't interested. So, we sent our son to daycare instead. I kept making excuses for him by saying that the job market was bad, or he was not feeling well, or he needed time to himself. After receiving a tough-love talk from one of my best friends, I realized that I was part of the problem for allowing this to go on for as long as it did by making excuses for him. Once I confronted him, it didn't take long to notice that he was lazy, selfish, and had zero interest in being a dad. We broke up shortly after that. Please tell your readers not to fall into the same trap that I did. If he looks, talks, and acts like a deadbeat, he probably is a deadbeat."

2—You ignore your man's bad behavior

This shouldn't be confused with the previous point. Making excuses for bad behavior is acting as if the behavior doesn't exist. Ignoring the behavior is when one silently acknowledges the behavior exists, but refuses to do anything about it. Usually, when a negative aspect of our lives is ignored, it comes back to bite us hard in the ass. Just think of it as a bill that goes unpaid. It will only get worse if it goes unaddressed.

Just a fair warning, you should be sitting down before reading this horrific story from Annette, a mom in California:

> *"I'll never forget that day for as long as I live. My daughter was seven months old and I planned a day of shopping and manicures with my sister. It was literally the first day I spent away from my baby since she was born, and I left her with my reluctant husband (now ex-husband) who was between jobs. For reasons unknown to me at the time, the man refused to change diapers, especially the poopy ones, but he agreed to on this day. When we arrived to the location (which was a two-hour drive away from home), he called to say that the baby had a 'really bad poopy diaper' and I needed to come home to change it. When I asked him to do it himself, he said he refused to handle one that was 'that bad' and I needed to come home to take care of it or else she would sit in it all day. Instead of arguing with him, I turned around and made the two-hour drive back. My sister was so upset that I was being such a pushover that she didn't talk to me for a month afterwards. I won't bore you with the remainder of the details, but after some deep self-reflection, I realized that I had put my head in the sand and completely*

ignored the signs that my husband was a deadbeat. He never wanted to be a dad, and I practically drove myself insane hoping that he would change. After months of counseling, we decided to divorce shortly thereafter. My advice is to confront the bad behavior when it happens. If you ignore it, the behavior will only get worse."

Crazy, right? I also know there are many of you thinking what happened to Annette would never happen on your watch. Maybe you're right. But as one of my good female friends once told me, "Men can make idiots out of the smartest, most well-intentioned women."

3—You feel like your man is your child instead of your partner

Cooking dinner, doing laundry, and teaching right from wrong is challenging when you're dealing with young children. Imagine doing that when you're dealing with young children in addition to an able-bodied man who requires the same treatment? He's not blind. He sees that you're exasperated and exhausted—he just doesn't give a shit. His laundry must be done, his sandwiches need to be sliced in triangles, and you clean up after him on a regular basis. Since he can't handle those fundamental tasks, it stands to reason that he won't handle any parenting tasks, either.

Kathy, a mom with twins, knows this all too well:

"My boyfriend refuses to find a job, he never washes the dishes or cleans up after himself, and there are times when I literally need to remind him to take a shower. He doesn't help at all with our twin boys, and at times

I feel like a single mom to triplet boys (including him). I complain, nag, and vent my frustrations to him, but he never listens. I'm thinking that's because he doesn't believe I'll ever leave him, because I've put up with this for so many years."

Unfortunately, Kathy is fed up with her man's childish behavior, but she's still around. That sends a message to the Daddy Doin' Nothing that her words are nothing more than noise, and he can continue along with his behavior without consequence. Don't we all know toddlers who act the same way?

4—You think that all men behave like this

These women know that their men are Daddies Doin' Nothing, but they don't do anything about it. Why bother trying to change these guys if they believe every dad behaves this way? Sure, they've heard about good, involved dads, but they've also heard about Big Foot and the Easter Bunny. Until they see one with their own eyes, it's just a myth. With an elongated sigh, they approach each day more exhausted and frustrated than the last, but they silently move forward without complaint, because at least their kids have a dad. Because in their eyes, a shitty dad at home is better than no dad at home.

Many of us know that couldn't be further from the truth, but when people come from a mindset that great, supportive dads are just a fantasy, it's not surprising they think this way.

Tatiana is a mom who fell into this trap, but eventually she saw the light:

"I enabled my ex by telling myself it was okay for him not care about our kids. I thought just the fact that he was physically there would be enough for them. I knew he didn't really want to be there, and I brushed that off as well. I kept thinking to myself that even a disinterested dad at home is better than raising children alone. I also thought every dad behaves this way (including my own father), so why would I want to go through the effort of starting over again to get the same results with someone else? Eventually, he left and I was devastated. It took a while for me to understand that our family was better off without him, and fortunately, I'm now remarried to an amazing man who loves our whole family to death. Now I know there are excellent men out there who love their spouses and embrace fatherhood. I just wish I learned the lesson sooner."

5—You feel relationships are not worth it

When the women in the previous four scenarios finally decide to leave, it's not uncommon to encounter other women who impede their progress. It could be their mothers-in-law, sisters, or best friends, but the messages are often the same.

"You should stay. Do you really want to be a single mother? Do you know how hard that is?"

"You really have no clue, do you? Good luck finding a guy who doesn't behave the way he does. Men are assholes."

"Your dad was the same way, and you turned out fine, right?"

"What kind of message are you sending to your children? Are you saying it's okay to run away at the first sign of a problem?"

"I think your expectations for your man are a little unrealistic. Do you really expect him to be Super Dad? This is real life, not a fairy tale."

"You know that women do most of the child raising, right? That's what I do for my family. Stop depending on your man to do your job."

Here's another reader example, and this one comes from our friend Lisa from earlier.

> *"After deciding that I was completely fed up with my relationship with Matthew, I made it known to everyone that I was planning to leave. Many people were supportive, but my mom was completely against it. She would call me cowardly for running away from my responsibilities as a mother and partner. She told me that my son would turn into a criminal and a drug addict without having a dad in his life. I'm her own flesh and blood, and she took the side of a man who unapologetically did nothing to support our family financially, emotionally, or spiritually. Granted, I left anyway, but her behavior damaged our relationship to this day."*

CHECK IN TIME

Are you currently enabling a Daddy Doin' Nothing or do you know someone who is? If so, it's nothing to feel bad about. At least you're mature enough to own it. The women who keep their heads in the sand will be the ones who will continue to live in misery while their kids pay the price. There's no chance in hell you will allow that to happen.

In the upcoming chapters we will discuss the amount of work that must be done in order to eradicate these clowns once and for all.

Let's get to work.

CHAPTER 7

ESCAPE ROUTE

DEADBEAT ISLAND

If I had millions of dollars of discretionary income, the first thing I'd do is start a cable television network with its own original programming—and one of the shows I'd create would eliminate the Daddy Doin' Nothing epidemic instantly. I'd call it *Deadbeat Island,* and here's how it would work:

A bunch of Daddies Doin' Nothing will get captured, put on an island together, and all they would have is crappy food, dirty water, and each other. The scorned moms (who happen to watch this all go down via satellite in a studio audience) get to choose the fate of these men in each episode. One week it could be watching them eat a meal you delivered to the island with your kids' poop mixed in as one of the main ingredients (just think of the movie *The Help* and you'll catch my drift). The next week it could include tying them up, blindfolding them, and quizzing them on their kids' birthdays. In the event they couldn't remember correctly, a NFL punter with a full head of steam could run up and kick them squarely in the hang low. The possibilities are endless.

More often than not it would include deploying the show's heroine—Gertrude the DDD ("DDD" stands for Deadbeat

Daddy Destroyer) to the island. Gertrude is mean, strong, and she's a black belt in the ancient art of Beating-the-Shit-Out-of-You. It's never a pretty sight once she finds the deadbeats. Well, if you're one of the scorned moms, I guess it's a pretty sight . . . but you know what I mean. I have no idea why this show doesn't currently exist, because it would be a freaking ratings juggernaut.

While I'm in the process of gathering my funds and soliciting investors for my cable network, we'll have to tackle this problem in a more traditional fashion . . .

THE HARSH REALITY

Women from all over the world are enduring daily doses of heartbreak from their Daddies Doin' Nothing, but how can they save themselves and their families? (Going through the motions and sucking it up for the sake of "family harmony" just isn't going to cut it anymore.) There is no family harmony when a guy like him is in the picture. It's just one heavy dosage of Band-Aids and blind eyes after another.

Kids know what's up, too. They may not be vocal about it, but they notice mommy slumped on the couch exhausted. They hear mommy snapping at them for insignificant things. They walk in on mommy sobbing in her bedroom and wonder if she's upset with them.

Remember, we're not talking about the deadbeats who run away from their responsibilities like little punks, because they can't man up and be dads to their kids. We all know they suck. Not to mention, nobody has to worry about getting away from them because they're usually impossible to find, especially when it's time to pay child support. Again I'd argue that a Daddy Doin' Nothing who lives inside of the home is much worse, because his children have the misfortune of witnessing his emotional unavailability all day, every day.

For example, let's say there's a little boy named Peter who is stuck in a household with a Daddy Doin' Nothing. If Peter plays on a baseball team with his best friend, Johnny, he may lay awake at night wondering why Johnny's dad goes to all of his baseball games, while Peter's dad makes lame excuses for why he cannot attend. Peter's heartache becomes amplified when he looks to his dad for support when dealing with bullies at school but is ignored, because his dad is too busy setting his fantasy football roster for the week.

Nobody is surprised when this leads to depression, illegal drug use, violent crime, or suicide. As you read these words, there is a boy looking to gang members to fill the fatherhood void. Somewhere, there's a girl having unprotected sex with multiple partners because it helps her feel loved by the opposite sex. Or maybe there's a kid who is so angry by the lack of love he receives at home from his Daddy Doin' Nothing that he'll pack up some semi-automatic weapons and open fire in an elementary school or shopping mall.

Is that extreme? Hell yes, it's extreme. This shit is *not* a joke.

Does that mean every child with a Daddy Doin' Nothing at home is going to become a felon, drug addict, sexually promiscuous, or a suicide victim? Of course, not. Some will surely rise above it, but others won't be as lucky. Even if one kid falls through the cracks due to a crappy dad at home, that's one too many.

PUPPY ABUSE

Let's say you were out and you noticed a dude kicking an innocent little puppy down a sidewalk. The poor animal was shivering in fear and crying out for help, but this horrible man kept beating it without showing any signs of remorse. What would you do?

For the dog owners reading this, I'm sure your blood is boiling at the thought of that. I'm not advocating violence, but I wouldn't blame you for wanting to thump the guy's skull with a blunt object.

Now let's add in a twist. What if you *knew* this man? He could be your friend, your neighbor, your cousin, or your coworker. What would you do then? Would you ignore it? Would you shrug your shoulders while believing it's none of your business? I doubt it. The fact that you know this man (or thought you knew him) would make you extremely angry or concerned, and that outrage would probably lead to a confrontation of some sort. If you're not the confrontational type, you'd probably tell everyone you knew within a fifty-mile radius about what you saw. Not only that, you probably would stop interacting with this person and potentially report him to the proper authorities.

Any guy who lives under the same roof as his kids and spouse, but shows zero interest in them is just as bad as the man beating up a defenseless puppy. The only difference is, in many cases the cries for help from the victims are muted, the scars are emotional. Many of us pass by Daddies Doin' Nothing everyday while carrying out our tasks, but we would never know, because they're so good at blending in.

Not anymore. That has to stop. Here's how.

SEE SOMETHING? SAY SOMETHING

If someone you know is in a relationship with a Daddy Doin' Nothing, you need to facilitate an intervention. Ask questions, get involved, offer tough love, and—most importantly, remind her that she and her kids deserve better. To hell with overstepping boundaries or feeling like a jerk for getting involved in someone else's business. Offering unsolicited advice when it comes to food choices for her kids? That's probably not okay. Offering unsolicited advice that will improve the emotional well-being for her and her kids? That's totally okay and necessary. More than likely, she already knows she's in a bad place and will welcome the talk.

Don't waste time asking why she had kids with him in the first place. She has them now and she needs help. Besides, none of us can sit here with a straight face and say that we haven't been conned by someone before. If you can, you're lying. It's not about what she did in the past, it's about what she's doing *now*.

The more people who bring this to her attention, the quicker she may wake up from the spell by her man.

DETERMINE IF YOU WANT THEM AROUND IF IT CONTINUES

Going back to the puppy scenario from earlier, would you still want to interact with anyone who abused an innocent animal? Chances are your relationship would be irreparably damaged.

Now let's say you were friends with this man's wife and she kept making excuses for his behavior.

"Oh, it's not a big deal. It's just a dog. It's not like he's doing this to humans."

Enablers make the same lame excuses for their men every day. They'll work a full-time job and put their kids in daycare because their husbands are too lazy to find a job or volunteer to be stay-at-home dads. These men will not be present for their families—physically or emotionally—and they leave their spouses alone to handle all of their children.

And what do the women say about it?

"It's not a perfect situation, but there's no such thing as perfect. It's cool."

Screw that. No, it's *not* cool. You want to know what's cool? Being a woman who refuses to have her children grow up around a crappy male role model.

The time to be tactful is over. Feelings will surely get hurt, but if these women insist on enabling the behaviors of these men, then we should immediately tell them how our choosing to spend time with them might change because of it. In other words, if there's any chance of a Daddy Doin' Nothing interacting with our kids, we will ensure it doesn't happen going forward.

Hopefully this will serve as a much-needed reminder to the enablers that we may love them, but the welfare of *our* children is, and will always be, our number one priority. If we were provided the choice of protecting our children or protecting the feelings of our enabling friends or family members, we would choose our kids every time.

BUT WHAT IF HE HAS ISSUES?

Maybe it isn't as simple as writing the guy off as being a lazy loser. What if he's struggling with addiction or depression? I'll let you in on a personal secret: shortly after graduating from college, I was clinically depressed. I wasn't a drug user, but it wasn't uncommon for me to spend twenty hours a day in bed hiding from the demons that tormented me for years. It was so bad that I considered taking my life on multiple occasions, but luckily, I didn't have it in me to go through with it.

Eventually those closest to me got in my face and told me that I needed to seek help or else they would walk. The words weren't empty, either. They loved me, but they were tired of the pain I put them through. That was when I knew I had to admit to having a problem, and I had to deal with it; so that's exactly what I did. I remember how much I hated therapy back then, but I hated being depressed even more—and I'm thankful that I stuck with it to be the man I am today.

If your man is a Daddy Doin' Nothing and he's struggling with something, I beg you to get in his face like my loved ones did for me when I was younger. In my situation, I was just a single, childless guy in my twenties, but the stakes are much higher if kids and a spouse are involved. If he takes the mature route of accepting he has a problem and attending therapy, then there's a chance your relationship can be salvaged. If not . . . well, I'm sure you know what has to happen next.

YOUR MOVE

In case you're wondering, I don't have an action plan for the Daddies Doin' Nothing who happen to be lazy losers, because I really don't give two shits about them; however, if you insist on me providing one for these clowns, I'll leave it at this: Man up and quit being selfish, punk-ass cowards. You're not edgy. You're not macho. You're not tough. Anyone who would prefer to sit on his jobless ass or spend countless hours ignoring his family is an insult to men everywhere who take the job of being a dad seriously.

But what if you're a woman reading these words and you're exasperated by the actions of the Daddy Doin' Nothing in your household? Take a moment to read this simple quote from self-help guru Jim Rohn:

"If you really want to do something, you'll find a way.
If you don't, you'll find an excuse."

What's *your* move? More excuses? I hope not.

Leaving him may not be easy. He's probably really charming, he knows exactly where your buttons are located and isn't afraid to push them, and he will tug on your heartstrings with his give-me-another-chance mantra of nonsense. However, doing what's right and doing something extremely difficult are often the same. Nothing that's worth having in life is easy. It's about doing what's best for you and your kids.

Speaking of your kids, if you don't want to take a stand for yourself and your happiness, what about them? Each day they're exposed to a lazy, emotionally unavailable meathead is a day they'll learn new patterns for how to behave.

Sons may believe that this is the proper way to treat women. Daughters may expect their future husbands to treat them the same way. I can pretty much guarantee that anyone reading these words right now would agree that's a big problem. If you have young kids, they can't simply get up and find a new family to live with. They're depending on you to make the best decisions for them.

Lay down the law and let him know that *he* has a decision to make.

ADDITION BY SUBTRACTION

Here's a fact: Daddies Doin' Nothing cannot exist without women allowing them to exist. Once ladies say, "enough is enough," these men will disappear like a fart in the wind. But as mentioned earlier, it's not easy for some women to leave them because these guys are so damn manipulative. If you're involved with one of the men described in Chapter 5, clear your head, take a deep breath, and think of one *good* reason why you're with him. You came up empty, didn't you?

If he's depressed or has problems with addiction, demand that he seek help immediately. If he refuses, then you should strongly consider refusing to have him in your life.

Let's assume he has no issues with addiction or depression. Do you think you can rehabilitate him? That's a noble thought, but if he's not intrinsically motivated to step up for you and your kids, do you think he can be trained to do so? Maybe. But you already have your hands full training your children to become valuable members of society. Do you really want to waste your time teaching an adult how to add value to your family when he contributes nothing? Only you can answer that.

If everyone reading these words takes time to shun Daddies Doin' Nothing as if they were puppy-abusing losers, chances are they would go away for good. Forget dating them, hanging out with them, or being friends with them. Sometimes the best move is to walk away.

Also, forget the antiquated stereotypes about raising children alone. Single parents raise some of the greatest leaders in history. Not to mention, imagine the pride you'll have when your kids become happy, healthy, successful adults, and you can tell them that you had the courage to raise them without the help of crappy male role models.

As parents, one of our biggest nightmares is the thought of our sons becoming Daddies Doin' Nothing, or the thought of our daughters marrying them. I'm not ashamed to tell you that it scares the hell out of me. But the tide is turning, and dads and moms are adopting a zero tolerance policy when it comes to these guys.

Good dads aren't hanging out with Daddies Doin' Nothing because they realize how horrible of an influence these losers can be. Moms are choosing not to spend time with their loved ones whenever a Daddy Doin' Nothing is around, because they want to protect their kids at all costs from negative influences.

The enablers are starting to look in the mirror and realize that they're a big part of the problem when it comes to this. Remember, if you're honest with yourself about being an enabler, that's a huge step. Doing something about it (usually leaving the relationship) is another huge step.

As the paradigms shift, future generations of moms will find themselves more attracted to loving, sensitive men who put their families first. Future generation of dads will realize that there is no chance of finding or keeping a good woman if they even think about exhibiting common Daddy Doin' Nothing behaviors. Paradigm shifts take some time to become permanent, but with your help and the help of others, we will get there.

It should also be noted that the Daddy Doin' Nothing army is a very small and pathetic one. Just picture a dying breed of weak men teetering on the edge of a cliff about to fall into a chasm of extinction and irrelevance. They just need that proverbial nudge that I'm sure everyone is happy to deliver.

Afterwards, we can wipe our hands clean and focus on the two versions of daddies that make up the overwhelming majority of fathers across the world. This is when it starts to get interesting.

SECTION 2
DADDIES DOIN' SOMETHING

CHAPTER 8
SOMETHİNG İS BETTER THAN NOTHİNG, RİGHT?

A COMMON LOVE STORY

Meet Jeff and Rachel. After being married for three years, they finally decided it was time to have a baby; however, the universe had other plans for them. When they visited the doctor for the first ultrasound, they noticed two heartbeats. Yep, twins—twin girls. Things were about to get interesting.

Rachel was a server at a popular chain restaurant and Jeff was a Sr. Accountant at the corporate offices of a clothing company. They lived comfortably in a major American city, but how would they survive when their family doubled in a few short months? Rachel knew instantly that she didn't want to put her babies in daycare, so she volunteered to give up her job. The thought of being the sole breadwinner for the family put an immense amount of pressure on Jeff. He made an above average salary, but he knew it wouldn't be enough.

When Rachel was seven months pregnant, Jeff was promoted to the director of finance overseeing thirty employees covering five different states. He was elated, because the title bump meant a pay bump. A significant one. He could easily be the breadwinner for the family while Rachel stayed home with the twins. Everything was working out perfectly.

In the final two months of Rachel's pregnancy, she saw less of Jeff than ever before. He worked his ass off at his job to ensure his bosses wouldn't second-guess their decision to put him in such a high profile role. That meant his ass was at work for ten to twelve hours a day, and when his ass was at home, it would be parked on his recliner. Rachel didn't mind. The guy deserved to rest after enduring long days at the office.

Then, Alexis and Amanda were born.

Rachel and Jeff couldn't contain their excitement when their baby girls made their arrival into the world in perfect health. Jeff spent the first two weeks of the girls' lives at home before he went back to work full-time, and Rachel couldn't wait to begin her role as a stay-at-home mom. She smiled and asked herself, "How hard could it be?" There's no way it could be tougher than being on her feet, serving annoying customers during the weekend dinner rush.

She was wrong.

Alexis was a great sleeper and Amanda wasn't. Amanda had a great breastfeeding latch and Alexis didn't. The end result was the twins were extremely fussy babies for completely different reasons, and that made each minute seem like hours. The only thing that kept Rachel going during the first few weeks was waiting for Jeff to come home each day to help out with the twins. Honestly, she would be happy just to take a ten-minute shower and eat a warm meal in peace.

Unfortunately for Rachel, she was in for a surprise. Jeff had very little desire to help out with the girls when he got home from work. The combination of conference calls, aggressive deadlines, meeting goals, and a demanding boss breathing down his neck at all times left him completely drained when he pulled into the driveway each evening. He needed to decompress and relax without dealing with his baby girls screaming in his ears. When he walked through the door, he wanted dinner to be ready, he wanted the house to be clean, and he wanted to be left alone.

In his mind, he *deserved* that treatment. Without his salary, the family would be living on the street. He reminded Rachel of that fact at almost every opportunity. And besides, what did she do all day? Watch television and eat Ben & Jerry's while the girls sat in their infant swings? He was tired of Rachel's incessant whining about how "hard" her job was. Jeff knew that only one person in the family had a real job, and it was him.

Rachel became depressed. She was so thankful for what Jeff provided to the family financially. They lived in a beautiful house, they had nice cars, and the girls had every material item they could ever need. But it wasn't enough. She wanted help in other ways. Her job was never ending. She couldn't clock out for the day. When the girls needed something, she was always the one to take care of it twenty-four hours a day, seven days a week. She was slowly growing insane.

Even on weekends when Rachel asked to spend an hour away to salvage what was left of her dwindling sanity, Jeff grumbled about how it's unfair that he has to "babysit" the kids on his day off. He thought, every day was a day off for her, and he was pissed that she was selfish enough to take away his limited free time to be on diaper duty.

For the first year, Rachel felt like a prisoner instead of a mother. Why couldn't Jeff see how burnt out she was? Did she have to install cameras in the house so he could actually see what she went through when he was not home? Even so, she knew he wouldn't budge on his stance regarding what real work was. Her role would always be giving baths, changing diapers, preparing meals, cleaning the house, and "other duties as assigned."

Rachel wondered if she was being unreasonable for asking Jeff to do anything with the girls. Maybe she needed to "Mom Up" and stop complaining about being tired. After a while, she came to the conclusion that every stay-at-home mom goes through extreme fatigue, so why should she expect that it would be any different for her?

Instead of speaking up, she just put on a brave face and kept moving forward for the sake of her family. That's what any good mom would do, right?

INTRO TO DADDIES DOIN' SOMETHING

In case you're wondering, Jeff and Rachel are still together and their twins are two years old. He still works at his corporate job and hasn't changed his stance on parenting. She still stays at home with the girls in a perpetual state of exhaustion. Because she knows he'll never understand what she goes through, Rachel just keeps her thoughts to herself.

If you're not experiencing your own Jeff and Rachel "love story," I'm sure you know someone who is.

In the previous chapters, we highlighted what Daddies Doin' Nothing are all about and how to deal with them. We can all agree that those men (if you want to call them that) have little to no redeeming qualities as spouses and dads, right? Well, now things are going to become a little more complicated.

What about the men who do *some* good work as dads and parenting partners, but leave a lot to be desired when it comes to being well-rounded, actively-involved dads? These men can be really good guys who just don't know any better, or they can be misogynistic jackasses who believe that a woman's place is in the home and a man's place is to make the money.

Welcome to the world of slowly-evolved dads, otherwise known as Daddies Doin' Something. Ladies, if you're involved with these men, some of the following scenarios will be quite familiar to you.

- Your man comes home from work, kicks his shoes off, and asks, "What's for dinner?" before he says hello to you or the kids.

- You and your man both hold full-time jobs outside of the home, but he expects you to do all of the cooking, cleaning, and child rearing.

- As a stay-at-home mom, your man makes condescending comments about how you spend your time watching talk shows and eating ice cream all day.

- While you're pregnant, your man thinks you're being a drama queen when you're vomiting non-stop, complaining of back pain, and being completely exhausted and uncomfortable. Not to mention, he expects you to be Super Mom to your other kids while you feel so shitty.

- Your man thinks it's beneath him to do any traditional domestic chores (dishwashing, laundry, etc.) or traditional parenting chores (changing diapers, preparing meals, reading bedtime stories, etc.), and would rather spend his time after work sitting on the couch watching television.

- He gives you a guilt trip or reads you the riot act if you try to go out with your friends for an evening. Because, you know, leaving the house with your friends requires his "approval."

- On rare occasions when you leave the house for an extended period of time, your man will tell his buddies that he's "babysitting" the kids.

BABYSITTING: THE DUMBEST THING A DAD CAN SAY

I honestly wish parents knew how dumb they sound when they say they're babysitting their own kids. It's impossible to babysit your own kids. A babysitter's role is merely to keep someone else's kids from breaking anything (valuables or themselves) for a certain period of time for a crappy hourly wage. That's it.

When a Daddy Doin' Something finishes working at the office—he wants to go out with his buddies for happy hour—he won't consider giving his spouse a break when it comes to watching the kids. She's the mom; that's what she's *supposed* to do. He completed a long day of *real* work, so why should he feel bad about kicking back and enjoying a few beers?

However, when the tables are turned and he's the one alone with the kids while his spouse spends some time away from home, he will make life extremely hard for her. She would practically have to beg him to "let her" leave the house. If he accepts, he would mention that she owes him for dealing with the horrific inconvenience of hanging out with his own flesh and blood alone for a few hours. And during that time he spends time alone with kids, he'll call it babysitting, because it's like a second job. For him, it's not enjoyable, it's not rewarding, and it's not a time for bonding. It's just annoying, and he can't wait for his spouse to get home so it will be over.

Why does he find spending time alone with his kids so miserable? Because when he's not in the office, he wants to rest, and it's impossible to rest when babies are crying and toddlers are tearing up his house. His end of the bargain when it comes to parenting is bringing home the bacon. Anything else is considered "above and beyond the call of duty."

News flash: Parenting is about *raising* children, teaching them right from wrong, offering discipline, being a shoulder to cry on, being positive role models, providing unconditional love and support, and doing all of this without pay. That doesn't sound like something any babysitter I know would do. From my experience growing up, I remember my babysitters plopping my two brothers and me in front of the television while they ate greasy delivery food and completely ignored us.

And maybe that's why these men call it babysitting in the first place.

THE GOOD NEWS

Hey, it's not all bad. More often that not, Daddies Doin' Something are excellent providers with a strong work ethic. It doesn't matter if they're driving trucks or running large companies, these dudes work extremely hard to provide for their families, and usually that includes enduring long and physically/mentally draining days.

Being a provider is important to Daddies Doin' Something, and it's what makes them feel fulfilled as men. If for some reason they get laid off from their jobs, you won't find them sitting on the couch shooting up zombies on a video game system for hours on end. They will be pounding the pavement or taking odd jobs to ensure the bills are paid and their families are taken care of.

Without their hard work and dedication to their employers, their families wouldn't be able to live in the houses they live in now, their vacations would be a lot shorter and closer to home, and their kids wouldn't be able to take part in all of those expensive afterschool activities.

When their bosses are riding them all day long, they grit their teeth and deal with it because they know they're doing it for their families.

Unlike the Daddies Doin' Nothing, these guys absolutely want what's best for their loved ones. The problem is, their definitions for what's best for their families is quite different from their spouses' definitions.

The dynamics of Daddies Doin' Something are multifaceted, but dealing with them hardly requires atom-splitting precision. It requires knowing who they are, why they exist, and what role you (women) have to play in their existence.

CHAPTER 9

THE İNCREDİBLY LOW BAR TO BE A GOOD DAD

UNDESERVED CREDIT

A few months ago, my wife and my two sisters-in-law went to Las Vegas for a well-deserved ladies-only trip, and the dads were left behind to spend time with the kids. After weighing our options, we decided to take our munchkins—all under the age of four—to the Aquarium of the Pacific in Long Beach, California, to introduce them to the wonders of marine life.

As the day progressed, people kept stopping us to say the following:

"You guys are some of the most amazing dads I've ever seen!"

"If only all dads could be like you."

"You guys make all men look bad."

At the time, we all took the ego-boosting compliments and moved on. However, as the weeks progressed, I reflected on that day and had the following deep thought:

"What in the hell is going on with our society?"

A bunch of dudes took their children out for some fun and exploration. So what? Do we *really* deserve credit for this? You would've thought we saved a pack of puppies from a burning building due to the level of praise we received that day.

Using another example, my twin brother went to a toy store to return a defective bicycle he'd bought for his daughter's birthday. When he walked through the parking lot carrying a bright purple bike, three different women approached him to gush over how great of a dad he must be.

It's important to be clear on what I thought were pretty obvious facts: a dad who takes his kids to the aquarium doesn't automatically become a great dad because of it; a dad who returns his daughter's defective bike to a toy store doesn't automatically become a great dad because of it.

A cute dad? Maybe.

A great dad? No.

This madness has to stop.

Is the bar for being a great dad set a notch slightly above "Deadbeat?" Since when did common parenting tasks become acts of greatness just because a man completes them?

In one of his shows, the iconic comedian Chris Rock said something that holds significant relevance, and I paraphrase: "I can't stand it when people expect praise for stuff they're supposed to do. For example, when people say, 'I ain't never been to jail!' What do you want, a cookie? You're *not supposed* to go to jail, you low-expectation-having motherf**er!"

Exactly.

Walking with our kids, playing with our kids, learning with our kids, and embracing the responsibility of being the primary male role models in the lives of our kids are things that dads are *supposed* to do. In my mind, giving praise to a man for taking his kids to the aquarium or returning a broken bike to a store is no different than giving him praise for staying out of jail.

The bar must be raised.

On the flip side, I would bet big money that if our wives took our kids to the aquarium that day without us, nobody would've stopped them to say our wives were the greatest moms ever. As a matter of fact, nine out of ten times, I bet, nobody would say a word to them.

I was driving recently and noticed a young mom with a double stroller struggling across the street with multiple bags of groceries. I didn't see one person offer to help her or say she's the best mom ever. Mothers rarely receive ego-boosting words; no strangers are taking pictures of them, as if the sighting was as rare as seeing the Abominable Snowman eating dinner in downtown Los Angeles—this happened to us at the aquarium—and no men are stopping them to say, "I wish all moms are like you."

But why?

Because many people believe that moms are just *supposed* to do these things.

This is a concern. Just because a woman gives birth to a baby doesn't mean she should bear the weight of every parenting expectation, while men skate by with the occasional diaper change.

The bar must be raised.

Offering effusive praise to fathers for navigating through common tasks is problematic, because it validates the behavior of Daddies Doin' Something.

Does he have a good job? That makes him a great dad.

Does he play the occasional game of catch in the back yard with his son? That makes him a great dad.

Does he occasionally take his kids out of the house without his spouse? That makes him a great dad.

I'm sure you can see where I'm going here.

THANKS FOR NOTHING

Oftentimes these men will expect a ridiculous amount of praise for completing ridiculously routine parenting tasks.

Let's say you have two young children under the age of five, and you took a trip out of town for the weekend. In doing so, you left your man behind to watch your kids, and he would be responsible for all meals, baths, activities, etc. If you're involved with a Daddy Doin' Something, he probably guilt-tripped the hell out of you before you left, and by the time you return home, one of two things will happen:

Outcome #1: Your kids will be found dirty, cranky, and full of fast food, because he has no clue how to effectively complete any of the tasks you normally complete.

Outcome #2: Your kids will be found clean, happy, and well-fed, but when you ask the, "Hey honey, how did every-thing go?" question, you better be sure to hire a professional violinist before he starts talking.

Daddy Doin' Something (long audible sigh)*:* "It went okay, I guess. Little Johnny peed on me twice when I tried to change his diaper, and Little Suzy refused to take a nap on Saturday. I'm soooooo tired. I hope you appreciate everything I did for you this weekend, because it was really hard. You owe me big time for this."

In the case of the second outcome, many ladies reading this probably think that he just described a typical Tuesday in your world. The sad part is, there's also a woman reading this who was in a similar situation, and spent time stroking her man's ego by thanking him for being such an amazing dad. But did this guy really do anything that qualifies as *amazing*?

The problem with these slowly-evolved men is an unwill-ingness, or a refusal, to realize that these tasks are a part of their job descriptions as dads. Instead, many times they believe it's something that requires their spouses to break out the heavy machinery to build statues in their honor.

Offering effusive praise to someone for doing the job they should be doing anyway can create a monster that will be extremely difficult to destroy. It's up to us to remind these men that they're doing something special by spending time with their children, but it should never be viewed as *something out of the ordinary*. Being a dad is way more important than sitting in a cubicle, driving a truck, or operating a business. Most importantly, being a dad doesn't magically stop once a man comes home from work. In many cases, that's when it gets started.

WHAT CAUSES THIS?

We know that setting the bar low to be a good dad is a problem, but *why* does this problem actually exist? Usually there are four major factors.

Factor #1—The Media

During a recent Super Bowl, a commercial for a popular fast food restaurant aired with a dad walking down the street with an infant strapped to his chest in a baby carrier. As he strutted through his neighborhood, attractive women swooned as if to say, "You are the BEST dad ever!" It was easily one of the most popular commercials of the entire Super Bowl that year.

I didn't like it at all.

The ad wasn't mean-spirited, and I know there are some of you thinking that I need to send a search party out to find my sense of humor. Don't worry, my sense of humor is still alive and well; but from a big picture perspective, airing a commercial to over 100 million people (the vast majority of which are impressionable young men) showing how a dude instantly becomes a Dad of the Year award winner and a "Chick Magnet" just by taking his kid on a walk sends a pretty crappy message. However, the media is known for spreading crappy messages:

Abnormally thin women define beauty.
Most young African-American fathers are deadbeats.
Women are weak and need men to save and protect them.

Most critical thinkers understand these points are completely false, but unfortunately not everyone is a critical thinker. In today's world, when people turn on the news or see a commercial, these stereotypes are constantly thrown in their faces. If they don't take the time to question what's in front of them, they'll just shrug their shoulders and think, "That sounds about right to me."

In regards to fatherhood, there were men and women who watched that fast food commercial and thought, "HA! Check out that dad with his baby. That's hilarious!" Meanwhile, that thirty seconds of shits and giggles perpetuate the archaic belief that men are *not supposed* to do these things; or even worse, it perpetuates the belief that taking a walk with a baby automatically turns a man into Super Dad. In other words, it keeps lowering the bar for dads everywhere.

Most importantly, let's ensure our kids don't fall victim to this nonsense. We don't want our sons thinking that they can strap a baby to their chests to "pick up hot chicks," and we don't want our daughters thinking that's all it takes for a dad to be considered awesome. Until it becomes a normal occurrence to see a dad completing the same tasks as moms without the added fanfare and hoopla that goes along with it, we will continue to see nonsense like this throughout mainstream media.

Factor #2—The Reactions of Women

Not all women are being called on the carpet here, but there are a few ladies who should probably think twice before gushing over the behavior of strangers. This not only happens in TV land, but many men also receive the same reaction in real life for doing what they are supposed to do as dads.

The women who do this mean no harm, and are usually very nice people offering up compliments to dads who are apparently doing the right thing. However ladies, if a guy looks cute while taking care of his children, and the irresistible urge comes over you to compliment him, simply ask yourself the following question first:

"Would I offer the same compliment to a random woman for doing the same thing?"

If the answer is "Yes," then fire away.

If the answer is "No," then you should probably keep it to yourself.

This is about evolving fatherhood. Either both men *and* women should receive statues and ticker-tape parades for completing simple parenting tasks, or nobody does. I'm in favor of the latter.

Factor #3—Extremely Convincing Men

If the media and random women on the street keep pumping up men with nonsense about how completing the most rudimentary parenting tasks makes them awesome dads, then they're going to start believing it. As a result, when wives and girlfriends ask their men for assistance, they're greeted with eye rolls, muttering, and bad attitudes.

They'll say, "Hold up. Didn't I just change a diaper yesterday? I already do so much for this family, and now it's not good enough for you?"

They'll say, "I took Little Johnny to the park on Saturday and I didn't receive any thanks. That's unbelievably selfish of you."

The monster is created. He believes his argument is a strong one, because he can't turn anywhere and not see other dudes getting praised for doing things many moms can do blindfolded. If you ask for help, at best you're being "selfish;" and at worst you're being an "ungrateful bitch who doesn't know how lucky she is" to have a man as good as him.

When some women hear this rhetoric from their Daddies Doin' Something, they think they're the ones at fault and not their half-assing men.

Factor #4—Portraying Dads as Idiots

Recently I saw a meme floating around the Internet that contained two pictures. The first one read, "This is how mothers are with their children," and it showed two well-manicured moms pushing their kids down the street in strollers with smiles on their faces. The second picture read, "This is how fathers are with their children," and it showed two burly dudes walking while holding their toddlers upside-down by the ankles.

For some reason lost on me, the meme went viral and people thought it was hilarious. The shocking part is that most of the people who found it to be so hilarious happened to be women. As I scanned the thousand or so comments, the majority of women reacted by saying, "Oh my goodness, this is SO true!" or "I love this! It's so funny and accurate!"

I have a painful news flash to deliver to any woman who finds something like this to be funny: you're part of the problem when it comes to evolving fatherhood.

I know, I know. It's just a joke. I should lighten up, right?

Sorry, I'm not going to lighten up on this one. Supporting asinine and completely inaccurate stereotypes of what fatherhood looks like keeps the bar for being a good dad really low. I've done a lot of dumb things as a parent and I'll probably continue to do them, but I promise you that walking down the street while I hold my daughters in the air by their ankles will not be one of them. The ridiculous part is that the women who find themselves laughing and sharing these memes with their friends are the same women who constantly complain about the fact that their men aren't putting in any effort when it comes to their children.

On a similar note, you don't have to look hard to find women laughing at a dad-proof baby onesie that has arrows pointing to the holes where the baby's arms, legs, and head are supposed to go through. Sadly, I wouldn't be surprised if a mom was the "mastermind" behind the idea.

Conversely, the women who are in relationships with great men who take the role of fatherhood seriously will see things like this, shake their heads, and think, "Really? People find this to be funny? My man is a great dad. He wouldn't hold our kids upside down, and he wouldn't need instructions to dress our baby." Right. No dad in his right mind would. So why the hell are people laughing at it?

Here's one of the few things Daddies Doin' Nothing, Daddies Doin' Something, and Daddies Doin' Work have in common: the overwhelming majority of these men are not idiots. They know how to properly push a child down the sidewalk in a stroller, they know how to change diapers, and they know how to read bedtime stories to their kids. The key differentiator is whether or not they're willing to complete these tasks.

DEMAND BETTER

Ladies, here's a call to action: Society needs you to expect more from the men enlisted with the duty of raising our children. Enough with giving over-the-top praise for changing diapers and trips to the playground, and enough with assuming all dads are bumbling buffoons, because it's doing much more harm than good.

That doesn't mean that dads shouldn't be thanked for being thoughtful when it comes to being involved with their families.

By all means, thank your husband for cooking dinner if you're exhausted. Thank your boyfriend for taking over the nighttime routine with the kids if you have to work late at the office. Thank your husband for taking the kids to the park for the afternoon so you can have a few child-free hours to regain your sanity. Thank your boyfriend for knowing the exact words to say to calm your rambunctious children when you're about to lose your patience.

I love to be appreciated. You love to be appreciated. We all love to be appreciated. The problem arises when we start offering up appreciation for things that we all should be doing innately. Not to sound like a broken record, but if there's a parenting task that you would rave over when a dad completes it—but wouldn't even blink an eye when a mother completes it—then you should re-evaluate if the task really deserves any amount of hoopla to begin with. Just remember the "Chris Rock jail reference" mentioned earlier.

Raising the bar for fatherhood isn't some trendy parenting nonsense. The well being of our children hangs in the balance. Is that overly dramatic? Not really. A good, involved dad can make a world of difference to a child, but it's the definition of what qualifies as a "good, involved dad" that needs to change in the minds of many.

CHAPTER 10

HOLD HER HAIR BACK: THE GOOD, BAD, AND UGLY OF PREGNANCY

Ladies, you don't need me to tell you that being involved with a Daddy Doin' Something can be challenging. He works really hard at his day job, and when he's home he wants nothing more than to be left alone. He's not changing diapers, he's not washing dishes, he's not cooking dinner—and unfortunately, he ain't daddying, either. Each day for you is extremely long, but if you're pregnant, those days are even longer.

Past and current behavior is the best predictor of future behavior, and for women who are pregnant for the first time, this is when you'll instantly find out what category the daddy-to-be falls into.

What if he doesn't give a shit about you or what you're going through? Most likely he'll be a Daddy Doin' Nothing. You'd be better off leaving and raising the child on your own at this point.

What if he understands that you're dealing with a lot, and puts your needs first as you carry his baby? Most likely he'll be a Daddy Doin' Work. We'll talk about him later on in this book.

What if he cares about you, but thinks you're being a drama queen when it comes to your pregnancy symptoms? Most likely he'll be a Daddy Doin' Something. This chapter is written with him in mind.

Some of you are pregnant while chasing around wild-ass children bent on destroying your house and whatever's left of your sanity. It's no secret that the quality of your man plays a significant role in making it through that forty weeks intact. Many Daddies Doin' Something have a hard time empathizing with the plight of the women they choose to partner with, because they are too busy worrying about what's happening at work. If you're stuck with one of these guys, go get him and read this chapter together. Don't worry, I can wait.

It's time for him to realize how tough it can be for pregnant women in language he can understand.

#1—Morning Sickness

I'm not quite sure why they call it morning sickness, because for many pregnant women, the feeling of misery goes on all day and all night long. When I used to come home after a good workout at the gym, the smell of my sweat triggered my wife's vomit reflex almost every time. In fairness, the smell of my sweat always makes her want to vomit all over me. But her desire to do so was much stronger then. Even when a pregnant woman isn't making out with her toilet, she still feels like she's suffering through the "Flu on Steroids" pretty much every minute of every day.

Memo to the Daddies Doin' Something

For starters, don't walk around your pregnant wife smelling like sweat (a lesson I learned the hard way). Also, don't trivialize it by saying, "It's not that bad" or "You must be faking it. Nobody can be this sick all of the time." That would make you an asshole of the highest order. In your younger days, you would hold the hair back of some girl you met at a keg party while she pukes into a nearby toilet or trash can in hopes you'd "get lucky;" so doesn't it make sense that you'd hold the hair back for the woman responsible for carrying your child?

The bottom line is to be as empathetic as you can, because hurling your guts daily is no fun for anyone. Again, if you want a reminder of what that feels like, just refer to your college days when you picked a fight with Jack Daniels or Jim Beam and got your ass kicked.

#2—Dietary Restrictions

Want a beer? That's probably not a good idea. How about some caffeine to help you stay awake? Yeah, that's probably not a good idea, either. There's an excellent sushi joint that just opened. Can you go there? Nope, you probably shouldn't eat that stuff. How about some cheese and crackers at a friend's party? Well, if the cheese is made with unpasteurized milk, you better stay away from it, too.

Can some of these dietary restrictions be dismissed as myths? Maybe. But are you willing to use your unborn child as a guinea pig to find out? Highly doubtful. Analyzing every piece of food or drink you put into your mouth for nine months gets old, quickly.

Memo to the Daddies Doin' Something

After a long day at work, oftentimes you'll come home without thinking about what you're eating or drinking. I get that. However, if you know that your pregnant wife or girlfriend craves something she can't eat or drink, take a ten count before taking it to your throat in her presence. If you're like most dudes, you probably like food. A lot. Not only does your wife like food, she's eating for more than just herself. Can you imagine how pissed off you'd be if you craved food you couldn't eat and there was a living, growing organism inside of you who also shared in your disappointment? It wouldn't be pretty.

However, when her cravings for peanut butter and marsh-mallows hit, don't ask questions. Just go to the store with a smile on your face and pick that shit up.

#3—Extreme Fatigue

In many cases, pregnancy saps every last piece of get-up-and-go women have, and taking a walk up a flight of stairs often feels as challenging as running the Los Angeles Marathon. Who knew that a baby the size of a mango could turn an adult human being into a zombie? Well, it happens quite often.

Memo to the Daddies Doin' Something

You have to institute the "forty-five-minute clock." In other words, when a pregnant woman tells you she's going to do something, you need to tack on forty-five minutes in addition to the time she gives you. For example, if she says it's going to take her thirty minutes to get ready to go out to the movies, it's really going to take her an hour and fifteen minutes—and when she's at the movies, she'll get up to pee no less than six times. The forty-five-minute clock is a tool that will save your sanity when dealing with your slow-moving pregnant wife. Just be patient with her and keep your frustrations to yourself.

#4—Inability to Get Comfortable

When Emiko plays horsie on my back, it isn't very comfortable. Luckily for me I can just tell her, "Daddy has had enough, baby. Let's take a break," and then she'll run along and find something else in our home to bust up. Unfortunately, that isn't the case for pregnant women who have tiny humans playing horsie on their bladders and other internal organs twenty-four seven. Sleeping is difficult, walking is difficult, sitting at a desk is difficult, and in some instances, even breathing is difficult.

Memo to the Daddies Doin' Something

There's not much you can do about her discomfort. She's going to squirm and complain, but that's all par for the course. Every woman is different—some will want you to massage their feet and others won't want you to be within ten yards of them. It's up to you to know how your spouse deals with discomfort, and accommodate her in any way possible. One thing I've learned is to not brush her off as being a drama queen or, even worse, offer suggestions to get comfortable (like a dude would have any idea how to make a pregnant lady comfortable). Don't do that.

#5—Short Fuse

Many of the pregnant women I've come across have short fuses and can be extremely emotional. For example, you can be at Babies R Us and comment on how you really like a certain baby stroller, and your wife/girlfriend will get pissed because she thinks you like the stroller due to the "attractive mom model" on the box. Maybe your wife will make you sleep on the couch because you wore a blue T-shirt instead of your lucky red T-shirt, and that's the "main reason" why her favorite sports team lost the game (this happened to a friend of mine).

Memo to the Daddies Doin' Something

There really isn't much you can do about this, except grab a straw and suck it up. No offense ladies, but some of the stuff you say when you're pregnant is bat-shit crazy, and there's no arguing with bat-shit crazy. Fellas, be supportive, nod your head, and do whatever she says. The lady is carrying your child, for crying out loud. She deserves a pass to act however she pleases.

#6—Strangers Touching You

I never understood this. Ladies, let's say you're *not* pregnant. What would you do if a random guy stopped you on the sidewalk and put his hands on your stomach to say, "Wow! How cool!" You'd slap the shit out of him and call the cops, right? So why do people think that it's okay to touch a woman's body just because she's carrying a baby? Almost every woman I know dealt with this when they were pregnant, and if you've been pregnant, I'm sure you have, too.

Memo to the Daddies Doin' Something

Start by not approaching women and touching their pregnant bellies. They aren't zoo animals, and they have boundaries that must be respected. However, if you're out with your pregnant wife or girlfriend and some random dude is dumb enough to put his hands on her pregnant belly in front of you, then you gotta do what you gotta do. I'm just going to leave it at that.

#7—Not Feeling Beautiful

I never understood this one either, but I know plenty of pregnant women who felt ugly while they were pregnant. I've heard it all:

I'm disgusting.
I feel like a whale.
I'm so fat.
I can't wait until this is over with so I can look like I used to.

Personally, I can't think of anything more attractive than a woman you love who is also carrying your baby. Not to sound overly cheesy, but pregnant women have a glow about them that just makes them really good-looking in my eyes (and not in a creepy, fetish way, either).

Memo to the Daddies Doin' Something

If there's ever a time to tell your spouse how beautiful she is, now is the time. Sure, there's a good chance she'll respond with, "Stop lying to me, asshole. I'll cut your penis off if you say another word to me," and that's fine. To be clear, it's not fine that she wants to cut your penis off, but you know what I mean.

Don't stop hugging her, kissing her, and offering sincere compliments to let her know how much you love and appreciate her. Whether she thanks you in return is irrelevant. Just know that deep down she appreciates your love.

#8—Dealing With All of the Aforementioned Shit in Addition to Your Daily Responsibilities

Memo to the Daddies Doin' Something

Think about the seven items listed on the previous pages.

Now think about all of those things happening while your spouse is cooking, cleaning, working a full-time job, and trying to wrangle your other kids.

Enough said.

You have to step up your game and help around the house, because whatever you were doing pre-pregnancy isn't enough now. Sure, you're busy at your day job and you're tired when you get home, but is there anything going on in your life that's more important than supporting the woman who is going to deliver your baby into the world?

If you don't cook dinner normally, you'll have to start now, or pick up some take-out on the way home.

Is giving the kids a bath your wife's job? Well, it's not anymore.

Do you hate doing laundry and dishes? Newsflash: EVERYONE hates doing laundry and dishes, but now you have to man up and take care of business.

Simply put, she needs your help more than ever during the months she's carrying your child. Don't let her down.

#9—Delivering the Babies

There are a lot of things in life that are difficult, such as juggling chainsaws while yodeling, or being the keynote speaker at the annual Ku Klux Klan convention as a black man. But I would put "pushing an eight-pound human through a small opening" (or two eight-pound humans, if you're having twins, like my mom did) at the top of that list. Having your belly sliced open to deliver said eight-pound human(s) is hardly a walk in the park, either.

I'm not going to insult any woman by beginning to pretend

as if I know what it's like, because I don't. I'll just go out on a limb and say that it's probably far from comfortable.

Memo to the Daddies Doin' Something

First let's review what *not* to do. Don't get drunk at a holiday party and tell your female boss with three young children that delivering a baby is no different than taking a dump when you're really constipated.

About seven years ago, a coworker of mine did just that. According to him, "Both acts include a lot of pushing, pain, and blood, so what's the difference?"

So, yeah . . . don't say stupid shit like that.

Also, I know it's not the most pleasant thing for a man to do, but you gotta be there during the Grand Finale. And by "be there" I mean witnessing *everything*. I was crouched down like Mike Piazza circa 1997 in full "catcher's mode" when my wife gave birth to both of my daughters.

Don't get it twisted—the act of childbirth is NOT beautiful; as a matter of fact, it's easily one of the most disturbing things I've witnessed in my lifetime. As I was holding my wife's hand when Emiko and Reiko's bloody cone heads came out, all I could think about was the movie *Alien*.

However, Mari never would've known, because I kept myself together on the outside, even though I was repeating happy thoughts to keep myself from puking on the inside. When I told her afterwards that I almost fainted eight times during the delivery process with Emiko, she said, "Do you think for a second that I really gave a damn about *your* feelings while I was trying to push our baby out?"

Well played. I made sure to keep my feelings to myself when Reiko was born.

So yeah, the act of childbirth is not beautiful; but when the child is born, it is truly the universe's coolest miracle. A living, breathing, crying baby who you would instantly trade your life for if it meant protecting him or her from harm. Now *that* is beautiful.

THE CLOSING PREGNANCY MEMO

Ladies, if you happen to be pregnant or plan on becoming pregnant—and you're involved with a Daddy Doin' Something who is too wrapped up in his own world to care about what's going on in yours—it's up to you to set him straight. If not, his lack of involvement and support will carry over to when the child arrives, and then your baby will be an additional victim.

Your man must have endearing qualities if you chose to have children with him. He probably has a strong work ethic, and in many cases, he's willing to take on the pressure-packed responsibility of being the sole breadwinner for the family. All of that is wonderful, but the act of being a true parenting partner begins the moment you receive a positive pregnancy test. I'm sure these women exist, but I've never met a pregnant woman who proudly boasts she's always on top of her game. Most likely, she's exhausted and experiencing some serious physical discomfort or emotional stress.

If you suffer in silence now, it will be ten times worse when the baby actually arrives and when he leaves you to do everything while he's at the office. There are a lot of women reading this who are dating or married to amazing men who don't need to be told to step up for their partners. They could have jobs requiring them to be away from home eleven hours a day; but when they are home, they still happily cook dinner, give baths to their children, or clean up the house to help take some of the stress away from their pregnant wives or girlfriends. These men are not mythical creatures. They exist in more households around the world than you know. If you're stuck with a slowly-evolved man, don't you think you deserve someone who puts *you* first? Especially when you're carrying his baby? Hell yes, you do.

Don't apologize for it. He should be there for you in any way that you need him to be while you're pregnant. The earlier you call him out on his not-so-helpful behavior, the better your chances are of ensuring he becomes a Daddy Doin' Work for your family. And you guessed it, being a great dad requires way more than bringing home a paycheck every two weeks. You need his love and support more than ever right now, and you should never be shy about asking for it if he's too clueless to offer it on his own.

CHAPTER 11

"WHAT DO YOU DO ALL DAY?" STAY-AT-HOME MOMS

HELP WANTED

We all know this woman. She could be your neighbor with the dark circles under her eyes who greets you with a half-smile as she staggers into her house with a crying newborn on one arm and a week's worth of groceries on the other.

She could be the stranger you saw at the mall trying to break up a "no holds barred" wrestling match between her two sons while all of the other customers gave her dirty looks.

She could be your exasperated sister who calls you in tears at 1:30 p.m. on a Thursday afternoon because she can't keep her three-year-old daughter from using borderline terroristic methods to separate the remaining sanity from her mind and body.

She could be your best friend who would strongly consider forfeiting her life savings if it meant she could enjoy twenty-four straight hours of her kids not touching, kicking, grabbing, or talking to her.

She could be *you*.

Welcome to the world of stay-at-home moms (SAHM).

Without question, these women have one of the most under-appreciated and misunderstood jobs on the planet.

MY INTRODUCTION TO SAHM

My dad was a young professor at a local university, and that left my mom to watch over three rambunctious little boys on her own while he helped mold the minds of America's future leaders. Even as a child under five years old, I remember how hard my mom worked around the house while my brothers and I concocted creative ways to maim ourselves and each other. She cooked, she cleaned, and she did laundry, all while going to school part-time at night to pursue her college degree. I remembered our craziness would bring her to the verge of tears many times, but we never relented.

One of us would break an antique vase, another one would make one of his brothers drink a cupful of his homemade "lemonade" (yes, it only had one ingredient, and by now I'm sure you figured out what it was), and another one almost parachuted off of our fifteen-foot balcony using a bed sheet.

I also remember the only thing that kept my mom from insanity was my dad. When he came home from work, he would be active around the house; he'd give us baths, read us stories, and play with us so my mom could wind down and relax. He understood that his work as a university professor was important, but his work as an involved dad and husband was—and still is—everything to him.

My dad clearly gets it, but that's because he's a Daddy Doin' Work. Unfortunately, the Daddies Doin' Something are the ones who remain clueless when it comes to being equal parenting partners with the women tasked with watching and raising their kids.

When it comes to the Daddies Doin' Something who are involved with SAHM, they can be divided into two distinct categories:

Daddy Doin' Something Version 1—The man who will help out every now and then, but secretly resents you for it

He's the one who comes home from work and rolls his eyes the second you ask him to do anything that has to do with his children or housework. He'll help you, but he quietly complains under his breath, "Are you kidding me? What have you done all day? Watch crappy daytime TV and stuff your face with junk food? How dare you ask me to change a diaper? I worked nine hours today at the office and I'm exhausted!" He usually doesn't have the balls to ever say it to the SAHM's face, but she's smart enough to know how he really feels.

Daddy Doin' Something Version 2—The man who clearly doesn't get it and will let you know about it

The demarcation line is clearly drawn in the sand. He makes the money. You clean the house, you cook the dinner, you do the laundry, you do everything that involves the kids, you get him a beer when he asks for it, and you have sex with him whenever he's ready. Have a problem with any of that? At best, he'll talk to you like you're a child. At worst, you'll get your nose broken. Well, it gets much worse than a broken nose, but you get the idea.

This chapter was written to deal with the men in Version 1, because there are a lot more of them than the men in Version 2. By the way ladies, if you're involved with a Version 2 man, you need to take the kids to a friend or family member's house and leave immediately. I'm not kidding. It's cool if he reads this, but you should email it to him when your family is a good hundred miles away from his caveman ass.

As you know by now, when Emiko and Reiko were born, I took four weeks off respectively from my corporate job to be a stay-at-home dad when my wife's maternity leave ended. The bonding experience was amazing, but it was also ridiculously difficult. Way more difficult than any office gig I've ever had. Having the added benefit of experiencing both sides of the fence made me appreciate the work stay-at-home parents (moms and dads) do every day; but as mentioned earlier, there are plenty of dudes who don't get it. They equate "being home" to kicking up their feet and watching television, so of course they laugh whenever their spouses complain about how hard their work is.

That's about to change. Telling your man how frustrated you are won't get you anywhere unless you explain it to him in a language that demonstrates the ridiculous amount of work you do to keep your family functioning effectively. We're going to break down many facets of an out-of-the-house job and a SAHM job, and you will feel more empowered than ever to stand up for yourself against the slowly-evolved man in your life when we're done.

Ladies, if you're one of the lucky ones who happens to be involved with a Daddy Doin' Work, smile and take pride in the fact that he already knows all of this. If you're a woman involved with a Daddy Doin' Something, feel free to invite him to read this with you as well. He may not like what's coming, because these words are directed at him.

THE HOURS

Damn, it's so hard working from 8:00 a.m. to 5:00 p.m. Monday through Friday. It also must suck on those really busy days when you have to stay in the office until 6:30 p.m. to finish a project.

Those two sentences were typed in "sarcasm font."

You want to talk *hours*? How does twenty-hour days sound to you? Weekends? Please. There are no weekends. When the baby is crying at 2:00 a.m., who's getting up? Is it you, Mr. Spreadsheet Superstar? Doubtful. She is the first one awake, the last one to sleep, and she does it every damn day, all damn day.

TOUGHER CLIENTS

I know, I know, dealing with the consulting firm across town can be really difficult. Especially Bob. That dude finds a problem with every proposal you put in front of him, he never listens to your suggestions (even though you know it will only benefit him in the long run if he did), and he constantly complains about everything.

Now let me ask you something: when you negotiate with Bob, does he ever puke all over you? Does he ever shit himself and demand that you clean him up before continuing with said negotiations? Now, picture that type of negotiation taking place multiple times a day. Depending on the size of your "consulting firm," your wife or girlfriend has to negotiate with more than one Bob or Susie simultaneously. At least you only have to deal with your version of Bob once a month.

VERY FEW BREAKS

Okay fellas, I get the fact that you're busy. Are you so busy that you can't take time to rest and relax for a few minutes during the course of the day? Maybe you'll take a walk to the corner Starbucks to buy a vanilla latte, maybe you'll check your social media accounts during the weekly budget conference call, or maybe you'll nap it out in your car at lunchtime. I don't care if you work in the mailroom or if the company is named after you; *every* person who works outside of the home takes breaks like these during the day, and you're lying if you say otherwise.

However, SAHMs aren't allowed this same luxury. In many cases, these women can't even take a break to use the toilet because there's a toddler causing a ruckus in the bathroom with them as they're handling their business. Could you imagine if Steve from accounting jumped around in the stall with you and screamed at the top of his lungs while you were trying to drop a deuce? That would be awkward, right? It's no less awkward if it's your own kid, trust me.

Additionally, during those rare times when the kids are napping during the day, there's very little time for a SAHM to rest. She's cleaning her house, she's trying to get through a bottomless pit of laundry, she makes herself a sandwich and coffee, and consumes both in less than forty-five seconds, and she periodically checks to see if her babies are still breathing. She hopes that she can take fifteen minutes off when you get home, but you're too busy bitching about how hard your day was spent sitting on your ass in front of a computer for eight hours. Fellas, the reason why this sounds ridiculous is because it *is* ridiculous. Man the hell up and hold up your end, for crying out loud.

THE COMMUTE

If anyone understands how much it sucks to sit in traffic, it's me. I live in Los Angeles, and I know that it takes an hour to drive five miles in this town during rush hour. However, when you're in the car on the way to work, there are so many things you can do to distract yourself. You can listen to the radio, catch up with your friends via phone, or simply daydream. SAHMs still have to navigate through the same nasty traffic on their way to the doctor's office, swim lessons, supermarket, etc. AND deal with a hysterically crying three-month-old who loses her mind as soon as you put her in the car seat, or referee two kids fighting in the back seat over who gets to play with a toy, or search for the location of the off-button on her three-year-old's "Why-Bot," or suffer through repeated "Mommy? Mommy?? Mommy!!!" "WHAT?!?" "Nothing" conversations.

There's no listening to the radio unless "Wheels on the Bus" is playing; there are no happy phone conversations; and if there's time to daydream, it's only to think of how to clone herself or to invent a way to sleep while being awake.

LACK OF ASSISTANCE

Can't figure out how to load the new proprietary software onto your company computer? Call the IT department. Need help with how to deal with a difficult coworker? Go to human resources. There's no 800 number for SAHMs, and most days they're working solo; they are human resources, IT, customer service, finance, hospitality, and health & welfare departments all rolled up into one extremely exhausted person. Yes, they can call up friends and family for advice, but how often are they stopping by the house to help out? Probably not as often as they would like. Not to mention when you get home from work, how often are you offering to help out?

SICK DAYS

You've done your best to avoid the nasty flu bug that's buzzing around the office, but the sucker finally bit you. You're miserable. Fever, chills, aches, pains, etc. You call in sick, and you spend all day alternating between sleeping and watching crime drama reruns on cable. It sucks, right?

Well, at least you get to rest and recover. What if that happens to a SAHM? Does she get to call in sick, too? Nope. She just suffers through the same fever, chills, aches, and pains that you suffer through, AND she has to watch over the kids while they destroy the house, AND they can't rest for a minute of it all.

I almost forgot to mention, having you at home sick is a nightmare for her, because it's like she just adopted another baby.

"Honey, can you get me some aspirin?"

"I'm hungry, can you make me a sandwich?"

"Can you check my temperature again? I think my fever's rising."

On a side note, I'll confidently state that women are a hell of a lot tougher than Daddies Doin' Something are on average. You want to see these guys look like complete wussies? Just wait until they get the sniffles.

LACK OF ADULT INTERACTION

You may not be best friends with your coworkers, but at least you're able to have an intelligent conversation with them about a variety of grown-up topics—last night's football game, current events, how much you can't stand Pete in the finance department, etc.

SAHMs are stuck in a vortex ruled by Patty Cake, *Dora The Explorer, Sesame Street,* and the Itsy-Bitsy Spider. Sure, they have their mommy groups and play dates, but since most of the conversations are centered around subjects like "What's the best diaper rash cream on the market?" does it really qualify?

Guys, do you ever wonder why your wife or girlfriend won't shut up when you get home in the evening? It's because she can finally speak to someone without discussing the amount of times her kid pooped during the day.

LACK OF RECOGNITION

You absolutely crushed it on a recently completed office project and you felt that your deliverable was near perfection. Unfortunately, nobody recognized you for the amount of time and effort you put into it. You're baffled at how your colleagues cannot see how hard you work every day for the betterment of the department. You come in early, you stay late, your work is always done well, and you don't even get a thank you. Instead, you're just "rewarded" with more work and more unrealistic expectations. You sit at your desk frustrated wondering how much longer you can tolerate this horrible working environment.

A SAHM involved with a Daddy Doin' Something is shaking her head thinking, "You just described my entire existence, buddy."

BEING MISUNDERSTOOD

SAHMs, have you ever gone out with your husband or boyfriend and someone (usually a man) asks you what you do for a living? After you tell him, how many times have you received the patronizing, "Good for you! What a busy job!" response?

Sure, some of the guys are sincere, but most of the time you can tell they're full of shit. Nobody has a more misunderstood job than SAHM. It's not all about daytime talk shows, surfing the Internet, sleeping, and eating ice cream until her hard-working man gets home. Many SAHMs are highly educated, supremely motivated women who *chose* to be at home with their families, not air-headed bimbos who haven't read anything in their lives other than Betty Crocker cookbooks or gossip magazines. Sure, men who work outside of the home can be misunderstood, too, but you'll never find a job where perception and reality are more diametrically opposed than with SAHMs.

INTENSE PRESSURE

You're a senior VP of corporate operations and you have a ridiculous amount of responsibilities at the workplace that the wifey just can't possibly understand. Quarterly numbers must be met, you have to find creative ways to stay under budget, and you're in the process of restructuring your workforce. Argh!!! There's so much pressure!

Here's my response to this:

Grow up.

Nothing irks me more than corporate bigwigs who complain about how hard their jobs are. I'm sure you're not bitching when that paycheck comes in, are you? Are you whining when you leave the office at 1:00 p.m. on a Friday to play a round of golf with Mr. Charlie and your other corporate buddies? Most importantly, did anyone put a gun to your head to take that job? You took it because you wanted to. If you can't handle the job, find another one.

By the way, you want to know what real pressure is? Pressure is knowing that if you're off your game for a split second, it could result in your most prized possession getting seriously injured, or worse. Don't believe me? One day, a very good SAHM friend of mine was so completely exhausted that she fell asleep at the kitchen table, and her two-year-old daughter grabbed her mom's piping hot coffee cup on the table and dumped it over her head. Her daughter is now eight, and her burns are hardly visible, but my friend's psyche will never be healed. Six years later she cries whenever she talks about it.

"I failed as a parent . . . but I was so tired. I just couldn't fight it. I was awake for twenty-six straight hours with no help. God knows I would never hurt my baby . . . but my body just shut down."

On top of that, her now ex-husband blamed her for everything. He said (and I'm quoting an email he sent to her after what happened), *"Your* only *job is to watch our kids, and you're too stupid and lazy to even get that right. Maybe I should throw hot coffee in your face before I go to work each morning to wake you up. I'm disgusted by you and I'm tired of doing EVERYTHING for this family!"*

If you didn't guess, my friend was married to a "Daddy

Doin' Something Version 2" as described at the beginning of this chapter.

She never received any help around the house. If she wasn't chasing around her two kids, she was doing some other domestic activity—because if the house wasn't completely spotless by the time her hubby got home, she would get chewed out. Twenty-six straight hours awake was too much for her, and her beautiful daughter paid the price for it.

Memo to the Daddies Doin' Something

If you screw up at your corporate job, at worst you'll get fired. And guess what? You'll just find a new gig. It doesn't matter what your role is at any company. If you're an employee, you're just a number. A faceless, nameless number. A SAHM is not faceless or nameless, and her "clients" depend on her for everything. If she screws up at her job, it could result in death or horrific injury to her beloved children. She can't go out and "just find new kids." Now *that* is pressure.

YOU HAVE NO IDEA HOW HARD MY JOB IS!

Even after everything that was laid out here, Daddies Doin' Something are constantly spewing nonsense to anyone who will listen.

"I have a boss that rides me all day long. It's hell."

"I don't sit in an office like a corporate sissy. My job requires physical labor and I'm exhausted when I get home!"

"This whole chapter is bullshit. You have no idea how hard my job is!"

You're right. I don't know how hard your job is. And not to be crass, but I really don't care. This isn't about you and your job; it's about your family. Whatever you choose to do during the day for work is irrelevant.

Do you think your young children give a shit that you had a rough day at work or that you're tired? They don't. If you don't believe me, just ask your exhausted spouse who spends countless hours trying to negotiate with them while you are away. More often than not, your kids just want you to be a good, involved daddy, and most reasonable people understand that it involves more than the money you bring home from your day job.

It's not only about being a good dad, it's about being a good partner for your spouse. Think of it this way: Let's say you have a job requiring you to work from 8:00 a.m. to 5:00 p.m. every day. Now imagine when you got home from work, your spouse required you to do the exact same work until you went to sleep, and sometimes required you to wake up from a deep sleep to complete it. When you ask her for help, she rips you a new one or flat out tells you, "No."

That would suck, right? You'd probably think your spouse is the worst person ever for being so damn selfish. That's exactly what she's feeling when you pull that crap on her.

NOW WHAT?

Ladies, if you're involved with a man who rolls his eyes at the thought of holding up his end of the parenting bargain after he completes a long day at the office, I hope you feel fired up and empowered to stand up for yourself and your children.

Do you know what his eight hours of work and your eight hours of work have in common? It's *work*. When you're both home together with the kids, doesn't it seem ridiculous that he feels as if his work trumps yours? I'm here to tell you it doesn't. If anything, the work you put in with your kids is exponentially more valuable and important.

Daddies Doin' Something are big on boasting about how "complicated and pressure-packed" their jobs are. In light of all of that noise, just take pride in knowing that if you and your man switched places for one day, he'd probably not make it until 10:00 a.m. before he grunted himself into unconsciousness. And after the pride wears off, you should be pissed, because there are millions of men who bust their asses at their jobs and are actively involved dads and parenting partners the second they walk through the front door. Your man just isn't one of them.

He needs to step his game up. Plain and simple.

Besides that obvious fact, don't think for a second that your kids aren't watching all of this go down.

Heather, a mom in Maryland, shares a story from her upbringing:

> "I'm eleven years older than my sister and five years older than my brother. When my sister was a baby, my dad would come home from work and refuse to change her diapers or feed her bottles. As a matter of fact, he would pay me five dollars for each diaper I changed. Granted, I was young at the time and I thought that this was the way all dads acted. He worked long days and came home exhausted, and since we hardly interacted (other than when he gave me money), I don't have a very strong relationship with him now that I'm an adult.
>
> "I can see my brother doing the same thing with his two kids. He never changes diapers, cooks meals, or even plays with his kids, because he feels as if his only

responsibility as a dad is to make money for his family. Anything that has to do with the kids is his stay-at-home wife's job. She's so tired and so miserable, but he thinks she's just being a lazy whiner. It's a terrible pattern, and I don't want my nephew to fall victim to it."

That simply cannot happen to your kids. Not on your watch.

The goal is to have the Daddy Doin' Something in your life realize the error of his ways and become more actively involved as a father and parenting partner. As mentioned earlier, many men in this category are completely oblivious to what stay-at-home moms do every day, and hopefully his eyes are little more open to your world than they were previously.

If you've tried everything (counseling, family/friend interventions, etc.) and your man doesn't come around, then you may need to make a really tough decision. As a SAHM, it's not very easy to pack up and leave since he brings in one hundred percent of the household income. But what's the alternative? Is suffering in exhausted silence better than demanding change and leaving, if those demands aren't met?

Tamara, a SAHM from Arizona, went through this, and she finally reached her breaking point:

"I was a stay-at-home mom raising my two-and-a-half-year-old son Marc while my ex-husband worked in hotel management during the day. He was a superstar at his job, but a complete dud as a father. His idea of spending time with our boy included buying him a tablet, putting apps on it, and sitting next to him on the couch in complete silence so he could watch ESPN and drink beer. Whenever it came time to go to the park, change a diaper,

or give Marc a bath, he refused. Not only did he refuse, he would yell at me for being lazy and selfish due to the fact that he was the one with a job. For the first year, I kept my mouth shut because I felt that maybe I was being too hard on him and I needed to back off.

"However, everything started to change when I met my new best friend Julie at a random outing at our local playground. She's also a stay-at-home mom, and when I complained to her about how tired I was due to being 'on' twenty-four seven, she mentioned that her husband works two jobs and is still the most actively involved dad on the planet to their two girls. He changes diapers, he does hair, he plays dress up, and he cooks dinner, and he does those things after working for twelve to fourteen hours straight on some days. It was at that point when I decided that I deserve more for myself, and Marc deserves more from his father. If this man works twice as much as he does, has twice as many kids, AND is an actively involved parenting partner and daddy, why can't my ex-husband?

"After having a true heart-to-heart talk about my desire for him to become more involved, he told me in no uncertain terms that his role is to make money and my role is to watch my son, and if I didn't like it, I could walk. And guess what? That's exactly what I did. After moving in with my college roommate, finding a job, and enduring an ugly court case, I now have full custody of Marc. I'll be honest, this was one of the toughest things I've ever endured in my lifetime, but I am so much happier as a single mom than I was with my ex-husband. There comes a time in life where one needs to choose to do whatever it

takes to be the best person he or she can be. Staying in that marriage was not it, and that's why I left. As I share the story now, I wonder why I didn't leave sooner than I did."

The moral of Tamara's story is to never settle. The universe has a funny way of taking care of people who have the courage to do the right thing.

CHECKING IN WITH MOM

Rewinding back to my childhood, my mom eventually went back to work, and she remembers the SAHM days as the toughest, but most rewarding of her life. My older brother Femi graduated with his masters degree from Harvard University, and was recently recognized as one of the hundred most influential African-Americans in corporate America by *Savoy Magazine*, my twin brother Shola is highly successful in corporate management, and then there's me, your friendly, neighborhood, Daddy Doin' Work. All of us are happily involved dads to our children, and we all list our mom as one of our best friends. Since it worked out pretty well for her, I figured I'd ask if she had any advice for the SAHMs out there.

"I'd tell them to always remember that it gets better. When you see your children grow up into amazing men or women, it makes the long days and nights totally worth it. However, it's important to have a true parenting partner as a husband. I know I would've lost my mind without your dad. After a long day at the university, he would always be there for you and your brothers. Being a dad never was something he was forced to do. He really

wanted to be one, and he was—and still is—the best dad I know. Not to mention, you boys had a wonderful role model when it came to being a great dad."

Ladies, I know the days are long, but please hang in there. Wear the SAHM badge proudly like Superman wears the "S" on his chest. When you sit there exasperated, wondering if your kids are actually listening to you, or if this whole parenting thing is worth it, believe me, they are, and it is. Not a week goes by when I don't thank my parents for the hard work and sacrifices they made for our family. And when your kids grow into adults, they will do the same for you. Will they do the same for your man? Not if he doesn't change his ways.

CHAPTER 12

CLIMBING THE CORPORATE LADDER COVERED IN SPIT UP STAINS: MOMS WORKING OUTSIDE OF THE HOME

THE STORY OF SAMANTHA AND JAMES

Samantha and James are married and have two sons together, ages three and one. James works in tech support for a large telecommunications company while Samantha does paralegal work at a medium-size law firm. It's gut wrenching for Samantha to drop her boys off at a daycare, but unfortunately they both need to bring in a steady income in order to keep a roof over their heads. James doesn't share the same emotions because he believes that working in an office and providing for his family is something that's wired into a man's DNA. He wishes he could make more money so his wife could stay at home with the boys, but that's just not in the cards for them.

For James, each day is relatively predictable; from 8:30 a.m. to 5:30 p.m. on Monday through Friday he helps people encountering issues connecting their computers, tablets, or smartphones to the Internet. Just like in any service industry, some of his customers are as sweet as apple pie and others are complete ass hats. The one constant is that he never works late and is always home no later than 6:00 p.m.

Samantha on the other hand never knows what's she's going to experience when she walks into the office. The lawyers in the office don't have children and they have a really difficult time relating to what she goes through as a relatively new mom. Some days she comes in to work in tears, some days she has spit up on her business suits, and some days she needs to drink near a damn gallon of coffee just to keep her eyes open.

On a good day she tries to leave the office by 5:30 p.m., but there aren't very many good days at this particular law firm. When a big case comes up (and every case is a "big case" to her bosses), she gets work dumped on her that usually requires her to put in extra hours. That would be fine and all, but she's the one who picks up the boys from daycare each day. The facility closes at 6:30 p.m., and if she's late, she's required to pay two dollars for each minute of tardiness. Since it's not unusual to be at least fifteen minutes late twice a week, it means she needs to drop an extra $30 for each occurrence. After a while, that adds up.

But wait a second. If James is always done with work by 5:30 p.m., why doesn't he pick up the kids? Because it's not on his way home, and he plays in a basketball league on Tuesday and Thursday nights, and he likes to enjoy the occasional happy hour, and he just needs time to decompress after a long day at the office. All of the above are legit reasons not to pick up his own flesh and blood after work, right?

When the work at the office is over, it doesn't mean that Samantha gets to rest. Dinner has to be prepared, diapers need to be changed, stories need to be read, babies need to be tended to in the middle of the night, and overall chaos needs to be prevented. As she uses everything in her power to keep the remaining marbles inside of her head, James is found chillin' out on the couch with a cold beer watching sports. Other times he can't be found at all because he's out having fun with his buddies.

Whenever she asks James for assistance (whenever he's *actually* at home), he rolls his eyes and complains about how he just wants to relax and be left alone. Besides, he makes more money than her, so that gives him a pass to spend time at home doing whatever the hell he pleases. It's a constant struggle for Samantha.

Big pressure at work with bosses who don't get her.

Big pressure at home with a husband who doesn't get her.

The light at the end of the tunnel is nothing more than a fast moving train ready to crush any remaining hope she has left for a stress-free lifestyle.

DIFFERENT CHALLENGES

Does this story sound familiar? It will if you're a mom involved with a Daddy Doin' Something while also working outside of the home. Back in the day, it would be rare to see a mom holding a career outside of the home, but in today's landscape, moms are crushing it as entrepreneurs, corporate hotshots, and senior leaders of Fortune 500 companies. Some of these women work because they love their careers. Some work because they have to in order to pay the bills. Some work for a combination of both reasons. Either way, the decision to be an employee instead of staying at home brings unique challenges after they kiss their kids goodbye for the day.

I know a lot about this topic because my wife is the president of a successful medical practice and I have a front row seat as she struggles with balancing work outside of the home and work inside of the home. Fortunately for my family, I'm a supportive husband and active dad who also rolls up my sleeves when I get home from a long day of work, and many Daddies Doin' Work are the same way.

But unfortunately, we're still talking about the Daddies Doin' Something here. These men work outside of the home as well, but they don't think about (or care about) how incredibly difficult it can be for their spouses to sit in an office away from their children for eight or nine hours a day. On top of that, these dudes turn their "work switches" off as soon as they get home and expect their wives to cook, clean, and be Super Mom while they relax on the couch with a cold beer.

If you're a mom who works outside of the home, you're probably a full-time employee for a large corporation, and I'll focus on the challenges that come along with that right now. Similar to the last two chapters, if you're romantically involved with one of these guys, have him sit right next to you as you read this together. Hopefully it will serve as a much-needed wake up call.

DAYCARE

When you work outside of the home and your boyfriend or husband does, too, this is an inevitable part of parenting. Since my wife and I both work outside of the home, we had to put both of our daughters in daycare when they were four months old, and it was absolutely heartbreaking for us. However, I know of people who had to put children as young as six weeks old into daycare because they had to go back to work to support their families.

Oh, did I mention that daycare is damn expensive? In Los Angeles, I've seen places that charge well over two thousand dollars per month for full-time infant care, and that's just for one kid. Imagine if you have more than one. If you're extremely lucky, you have family nearby to watch your children while you're at work, but many don't have that luxury.

Most importantly, these moms have to deal with the fear of leaving their extremely vulnerable loved ones in the care of strangers. We're blessed to have awesome daycare providers, but we're painfully aware of one fact: unless your daycare facility is tricked out with video cameras, no parent truly knows how their daycare providers are treating their children.

Are they too rough with your kids? Are they yelling at them for minor things? Are they suffering in poopy diapers for hours until someone finally decides to change them? Are they eating nasty, unhealthy food? Are they thrown into a dark scary room at naptime to cry themselves to sleep while they're screaming for their mommies and daddies?

Many of these moms never know the answers to these questions, but it doesn't stop them from worrying every day when they leave their kids with non-family members. Even worse, when these women are involved with Daddies Doin' Something, they can never voice their concerns without being brushed off for being whiny and oversensitive. Their men will just shake their heads and sigh, "Get over it. Little Johnny is home in one piece. What's the big deal?" Feeling the fear is bad enough. Not having support at home to help cope with that fear is even worse.

UNEXPECTED ABSENCES

Uh oh. Daycare calls you with some bad news. Little Johnny is sick with the flu and they need you to pick him up immediately, because as the provider snaps, "We run a daycare center, not a doctor's office."

Unfortunately, you have an important meeting to attend in an hour where you're tasked with presenting the company's marketing strategy for the next quarter. Many senior executives will attend the meeting, and you are the only person who knows enough about the subject matter to deliver this information. For some lame reason, your Daddy Doin' Something husband refuses to pick him up, you have no friends or family available to help out, and you make the uncomfortable realization that you are the only person who can get him.

You have a choice: Pick up your sick kid and potentially jeopardize your career by skipping this meeting, or have the daycare providers leave little Johnny on the curb until the meeting's over and hope that he doesn't get kidnapped or have his fever shoot through the roof by the time you get him.

Yes, the choice is a no-brainer, and no daycare provider would leave a kid on a curb—I was only kidding. But that doesn't make it any easier for these moms to deal with. Unexpected shit like this happens to them all of the time. When they have important meetings or deadlines at work, they drive into the office chanting, "Please don't let anything happen with my kids . . . please don't let anything happen with my kids," because they know they'll have to deal with extremely uncomfortable conversations with their bosses and colleagues if they have to leave. It's even harder for the hourly workers, because if they're not at work, they don't get paid. Yes, the priority is to always take care of our children, but it ain't easy when your wallet takes a hit in the process.

Again, scenarios like this are much easier to deal with for ladies who are involved with men who happily step up like they are supposed to. No chance of that happening with a Daddy Doin' Something, unfortunately. Even though his spouse works a demanding job outside of the home as well, it's not his responsibility to pick up little Johnny. He's still stuck in the stone ages by believing his spouse is responsible for everything that is kid-related, no matter what's going on for her at the office.

DEALING WITH A BOSS WHO DOESN'T GET IT

I read a statistic that ninety percent of people who are unhappy with their jobs list their immediate supervisors as the primary reason for it. When these moms become unhappy with their bosses, it's usually due to the fact that they don't understand what they go through every day.

She could stumble into her office like a zombie because she had three total hours of sleep the night before (not three consecutive hours, either) due to an extremely cranky baby, and her boss relentlessly rides her for not "bringing the energy like the other team members."

Of course, her other team members don't have kids, but her boss isn't interested in her "excuses." All he cares about is meeting his department goals, and if she isn't onboard with helping him, then she's against him.

What if she needs to leave early to take her daughter to the doctor? He'll make her feel like the worst employee in the world (even though she's probably the best mom in the world).

What if she can't stay late to finish the project? He'll take a "mental note" of it, and crush her for not being a team player when it's time for her annual performance review.

What if she wants to request vacation time? He'll deny it because she's "already taken enough time off" to take care of her kids.

What if she needs to take a call from her son's teacher? Her boss will stand over her while she's on the phone and put her on a written warning for taking too many "personal calls" during company hours.

Don't think for a second that this is hyperbole. These bosses actually exist. Actually, I'm sure many of the moms reading this have experienced a lot worse from their bosses.

Bearing the weight of all of the parenting responsibilities, namely, attending parent-teacher conferences, leaving early when kids are sick, taking calls from daycare providers, etc.—in addition to having a boss from hell—is literally enough to drive these women completely bat-shit crazy.

If you have a boss who understands what it's like to juggle the responsibilities of being a mom and an employee and will gladly cut you some slack when you need it, then consider yourself very lucky.

MOM GUILT

I saved the worst for last. I have a very good friend who has three young children (a toddler and four-month-old twins), and I asked her what she thought the toughest thing was about leaving her kids to go to work each day. She paused, tears welled up in her eyes, and she said, "Without question, it's the Mom Guilt. I just can't shake it."

What is Mom Guilt, you ask?

Mom Guilt is knowing her kids could be saying their first words, taking their first steps, etc. in front of daycare providers instead of them.

Mom Guilt is keeping her cool when the daycare provider says, "You won't believe the cute thing your kid did today!"

Mom Guilt is lying to the daycare provider when her child is sick and dropping him off there anyway because she absolutely can't miss work today.

Mom Guilt is sitting at work in tears wishing she could hug her children instead of dealing with the jerks around her.

Mom Guilt is knowing her kids may feel resentment toward her when she spends long hours at work, no matter how much she tries to diffuse it.

Mom Guilt is being devastated when her children say they would rather be around their daycare providers instead of her.

I think you see where I'm going with this. Mom Guilt is no joke. Many moms I know feel it. If you're a mom with young children in daycare, you probably feel it, too.

NO REST FOR THE WEARY

After dealing with all of the challenges described in this chapter, nobody would be surprised if these moms come home mentally and physically exhausted. But when they are partnered with Daddies Doin' Something, walking through the front door means walking into chaos at every corner. Diapers need changing? She's the one to do it. Dinner needs to be made? She's in the kitchen. Kids need bathing? She's rolling up her sleeves and getting wet.

By the time the kids are asleep, she's ready to pass out on the floor; but where's her man during all of this? He's relaxing on the couch ignoring everyone around him. His spouse gets no sympathy for what she's going through because that's what is *expected* of her as a mom and wife. It's a damn joke.

Ladies, if you're dealing with any of these issues, I have to hit you over the head with some real talk. It's going to be extremely difficult for you to sustain this. You can try if you want to, but you're guaranteed to lose your productivity at work, your engagement level with your kids, and, most importantly, your mind, if serious change doesn't occur. We know you're a superstar at the office and Super Mom at home, but even superheroes need support in their lives.

CHAPTER 13

IS GOOD ENOUGH GOOD ENOUGH?

By now you know how Daddies Doin' Something operate, and if you're involved with one, a lot of what you've read is similar to what takes place in your household. These guys are by no means in the same neighborhood as the clowns we reviewed in the Daddy Doin' Nothing section, but they also aren't in the same neighborhood as the amazing men we'll talk about in the upcoming Daddy Doin' Work section either. If parenting were a university, Daddies Doin' Something would be the "C" students.

If you have a Daddy Doin' Something in your life, I hope you read the previous few chapters with him. If so, what was his initial reaction? Did he take it to heart and say he'll change for the sake of your family? Or was everything met with heavy sighing, head shaking and eye rolling? If it's the former, you should rejoice because he probably wasn't aware of how his behavior was impacting you and your family. If it's the latter . . . well, it means we have more work to do.

If he thinks everything he read was bullshit, that's probably because he lacks the ability to take the perspective of another person. If your partner lacks empathy, it's going to be very challenging to get him to understand what you're going through. He hears about your cries for help, but everything you say is greeted by a "Yeah, but."

"Yeah, but I'm tired, too. I work really hard at the office."

"Yeah, but you're the mom. You *should* be doing these things."

"Yeah, but I don't see the other moms complaining nearly as much as you do."

If having him see the world through a mom's mindset isn't working, we'll have to find out how seriously he wants to be a good, involved dad.

CAREER LOYALTY

A Daddy Doin' Something's career is an enormous portion of his life, and more often than not it's what defines him and makes him feel like a man (which is pretty sad, actually). In most cases he either loves his job and puts a crazy amount of energy into it, which leaves no energy left for your family, or he hates his job and wants to be left alone to decompress as soon as he walks through the front door. Regardless, it sucks if you're involved with this guy, because the end result is that his feelings about his job affects his ability to pull his weight as a dad.

What he's painfully unaware of is how to use the most valuable resource we have to give—time. As a matter of fact, it's the only resource we can never get back once we give it. Our babies will only be the age they are right now, *right now*. The days of teething, potty training, sleeplessness, and toddler tantrums will be traded in for college and dating before we can blink an eye, and we'll wish we had those days back. I can't speak for most men, but while I sure as hell can't remember what my first conference call or first performance review at work was like, I absolutely can remember my daughters' first words and first steps as if they occurred yesterday.

He simply needs to understand that his primary job is being a dad. A nurturing, caring, loving, attentive dad. Jobs come and go, but his kids will always be there, and he needs to realize that before he looks back on his life with a shit load of regret.

Here's a story I like to share with people who have their priorities out of order. Many years ago, a man named Larry was in charge of the human resources department for a company I used to work for. You know how people jump from job to job every few years once they outgrow their current position? Not Larry. This cat wasn't going anywhere. As a matter of fact he started working at this company as a college intern, and by the time I arrived, he was entering his seventeenth year.

I was single and in my mid-twenties, so I didn't really have much of a frame of reference in regard to work-life balance, but even my clueless self knew that something didn't seem right about this dude's attitude. He was in the office all of the time, and by "all of the time," I mean it wouldn't be surprising to see him working eighteen-hour days. I knew this because the gym I went to was a block away from my office, and I'd see his car in the parking lot and a light on in his second floor office as early as 5:00 a.m. and as late as 11:00 p.m. whenever I drove by. Weekends included.

Larry wasn't a single guy like me. When I met him, his wife was a SAHM, and they had two young daughters aged four and one. After we got to know each other a bit, I finally asked him the question: "You spend a lot of time here at the office. Doesn't your family miss you or need you at home?" Larry put his hand on my shoulder and laughed, "Doyin, I love my job

and I'm extremely loyal to this company. Having career loyalty to your employer is extremely important and I hope you
demonstrate the same loyalty that I have." I knew I had to tread
lightly because he was a big wig and I was just a peon with a
crappy hourly wage, but the dude didn't answer my question. I
wanted to know why in the world does he choose spend close
to eighty hours a week at work instead of with his family.

So I tried again. "Not to pry, but I'm assuming your wife
and kids are okay with you spending all of your time here then,
right?" He gave me a look as if I was a complete moron, "Of
course, my wife is okay with it. I'm sure she wouldn't be okay
with living on the street without my salary. I'm also sure that
my kids are happier being around their mom instead of at some
daycare. It's called being a good dad, my friend. You'll figure it
out soon enough." That was the end of our conversation, and I
went home for the night. Like I said, I was single with no kids.
I assumed that's how all executives with wives and kids acted.

Larry's direct supervisor was one of the senior vice presi-
dents, and whenever he happened to be in our office, I would
always hear Larry talk about how loyal he was to him and the
company. His boss would always eat it up and respond by saying how valued of an employee he was, and this dog and pony
show would continue every time they crossed paths.

Then, one day it happened.

On his way into the office on a Tuesday morning, he suffered a massive heart attack and died in the ambulance on the
way to the hospital. His wife and kids were absolutely devastated. The guy was freaking thirty-nine years old. Thirty-nine-
year-olds shouldn't be dying of heart attacks. He had children
the same ages as mine are now. As shocking as his death was to
many, I remember the reaction of his direct supervisor as being

even more disturbing. By Thursday of that same week—less than two full days after his death—he was conducting interviews for Larry's job, had his office cleaned out, and acted as if it never happened.

Remember, this is the guy who gave his entire adult life to this company. He broke his back for the company. He slept in his office to finish projects for the company. He sacrificed all of his time with his wife and kids for the company. Why? Because he was *loyal* to the company. How did that loyalty work out for him? Seventeen years was forgotten about in less than forty-eight hours.

Of course, many would argue that a large business needs to run efficiently and they can't spend months mourning an employee's passing, but the way management just swept his death under the rug and kept moving was an eye-opener for me. Companies are rarely as loyal to people as they are to the bottom line. From that point forward I always worked extremely hard when I was in the office, but my loyalties were always with my loved ones before my employers. Larry was a damn superstar at his job. If he could be forgotten so quickly and easily, imagine what they would do to somebody like me?

I'm not sure how Larry's family is doing these days, but I know that his girls won't remember much of him because he was never at home. Even today I think of him and wonder, if he could do it all over again would he choose to be more loyal to his job than to his wife and daughters. I wonder if his definition of being a good dad has changed now that he's up in heaven. Obviously I don't have the answers to those questions, but I'm sure there is a woman reading this who's involved with a man just like Larry, and it's my sincere hope that it doesn't end the same way for her as it did for his family.

If your man sounds like Larry, share this story with him. In a world where people always complain about how much they despise their jobs, it's awesome that your guy loves his. But at what cost? Does he put all of his passion into a job that can be taken away from him at a moment's notice leaving an empty tank for the children and spouse who depend on him and need him? If so, I simply cannot wrap my head around that.

Put it in terms that he can understand. Ask him flat out if his projects at work are more important than being a present parenting partner. Remind him that no employer will ever be as loyal to him as you and your kids are. Remind him that each day that passes when he ignores the kids is a missed opportunity to create memories that will last a lifetime.

In most instances he can leave work at a reasonable hour to spend quality time with the kids. Surely, he can change diapers, read stories, deliver bottle feedings when he gets home. If he goes above and beyond for a bunch of strangers and acquaintances at the office, why can't he do what he's supposed to do as a dad when he gets home? Don't ask him to be the dad his kids deserve; confidently demand it. I'm here to tell you that there are men who work ridiculous hours at the office or have multiple jobs and still put their families first by being actively involved. Why can't he Dad Up and do it, too?

CAREER LOATHING

Then there's the guy who hates his job or just simply goes through the motions when at work. You don't have to worry about him putting in a minute longer at the office than he absolutely has to, but the time he spends is so draining that he can't handle a moment of additional stress when he gets home. He needs peace and quiet. But shit, doesn't he realize you need peace and quiet, too? Why is it okay for him to spend one hundred percent of the time on the couch relaxing after work while you can't clock out until the kids go to bed? That hardly seems fair.

Many Daddies Doin' Work are employees at jobs they absolutely hate, but what makes them special is they don't take it out on their families. Instead, they look forward to the moment they walk inside to give their kids big hugs and kisses. They live for their families. Nothing is more important. I can always tell when a dude enjoys being a dad after he endures a particularly difficult day at the office. If his first thought is, "I don't want to talk to anyone and I don't want to do anything when I get home," you probably know he's going to be a Daddy Doin' Something. The sad part is, many young children don't understand the concept of work and having a horrible day. All they understand is their hero lets them down every time he brushes them off or ignores them.

Similar to the dads who love their jobs, you need to flat out demand him to step up his game. If he's so miserable at work, he needs to put his big boy pants on and find another job that will make him happier. So many women whom I've encountered in this situation are afraid to speak up for fear they'll upset their men. No matter what you do for work (SAHM or working outside of the home), your job is stressful. It's not okay that he thinks he can pawn off all of the parenting duties on you because you have a vagina. If a fifty-fifty split of responsibilities doesn't occur, you'll either lose your mind or you'll become extremely resentful about it. None of those outcomes benefit you or your children.

THE BEST RESTAURANT IN TOWN

So here are the million dollar questions should you be involved with a Daddy Doin' Something: are you cool with the way things are? Is "good enough" good enough for you?

Think about it this way. There's an amazing restaurant that opened up on the other side of town. Everybody who eats there says it has the best food ever, it's kid-friendly, and the prices are extremely reasonable. After listening to all of the hype, you finally decide to take your kids there to find out what the big deal is. Since your man is a Daddy Doin' Something, he decides to stay home so he can watch sports alone without you or the kids getting in his ear. No surprise there.

All of your friends recommend the steak for the adults and the mac and cheese for the kids. Apparently, the knife cuts through the meat like butter and has flavor like nothing else on the planet. The owner of the restaurant says that he knows of at least fifty patrons who used their mac and cheese to help potty train their kids. Put differently, the parents bribed them by saying if they use the potty, they can go back to the restaurant and eat some more of their cheesy goodness, and it worked every time. Without hesitation, you order the steak for yourself and mac and cheese for your three-year-old daughter and two-year-old son. You and your kids haven't been more excited for a meal in your lives.

After the server places the meals on your table, you notice something. The steak doesn't look quite right. It smells good, but it's overcooked and isn't very easy to cut. The mac and cheese is lukewarm and pasty, and your kids give you the unmistakable, there's-no-way-I'm-eating-that look. You're confused. Is this the food everyone is raving over? It's not like a rabid junkyard dog crapped on your plates, but it also isn't the world's greatest grub. It's just extremely mediocre. You stand up and notice the family next to you ordered the same thing you did, except for their steak was thick, succulent, and juicy, and the mac and cheese was extra creamy and cheesy. Just to ensure you're not losing your mind, you ask the mom what she ordered for her family and she confirmed it's the same.

Instead of raising a stink about it, you choke down your rubbery steak and make your kids eat their cold pasta. Even though the family next to you paid the exact same price and is enjoying a better version of the meals, you rationalize it by saying, "So we experienced a little bad luck. Big deal. We've all eaten worse food than this. It's good enough."

Does this sound like something you would ever do? Everyone around you can't stop talking about how great this restaurant is and you're just going to accept the half-assed culinary attempt on your table as being "good enough" for you and your kids? If you're like me, it would be a no-brainer to approach the server and request a better version of the food you ordered.

So, why do some moms shrug their shoulders and accept the Daddies Doin' Something in their lives for being "good enough" for their families? Sure, these guys aren't deadbeats, but these women know there are great men out there who understand that paying bills is only a small part of what they bring to the table as dads, but for some reason they don't believe they deserve it. Instead, lame excuses are offered just like at the restaurant.

"He works so hard. I just need to suck it up."

"If I stay at home, then I shouldn't expect him to do anything with the kids when he returns from work."

"His role is to make money and my role is to take care of the kids. Sure, I'm tired, but so is he. Every mom goes through this."

"At least he has a good job. It's not like he's sitting on his ass at home surfing the Internet all day. I need to cut him some slack."

"Moms are just better at parenting than dads. I'm not going to force him to do things that don't come naturally."

So, standing up for your family at a restaurant is totally reasonable and expected, but doing so when it comes to the primary male role model in your kids' lives is not? We all know that makes no sense whatsoever. Speaking of the kids, the thought of you eating a subpar meal is one thing, but when your babies are involved, it's another story. Seeing the disappointment in the eyes of your children is enough to set off your Mama Bear alarm, which will prompt you to confidently confront the chef and say, "Look at what you prepared for my kids. Do you think this is okay? Every other child is enjoying amazing mac and cheese and that's what my children deserve as well." No way in hell are you leaving that establishment without your kids eating the amazing meal every other kid is enjoying.

Here's one of my all-time favorite quotes from a Dr. Seuss classic, *The Lorax:* "Unless someone like you cares a whole awful lot, nothing is going to get better, it's not."

Who knew that an imaginary character could drop such knowledge? Until we give enough of a damn to do something to improve our own lives and the lives of our children, nothing will ever get better. Don't sleepwalk through life by settling for less than what you deserve for a minute longer.

When a man chooses to be involved in a child's life, that

child should expect him to be amazing. No excuses. No exceptions. And if you're a woman involved with a slowly-evolved man, you should confront him with the same confidence that she would approach the employees at a restaurant when delivered a mediocre meal. If you won't do it for yourself, think about your children. I know for a fact that you care about them a whole awful lot. If you don't stand up for them, then who will?

You may be one who believes that your religion or faith requires you to abide by "traditional gender roles;" meaning, men work outside of the home, while women raise the children. Ladies, I'm not here to speak negatively about anyone's religion, but I'll simply ask if your current setup positively serves you and your family. If the answer is yes, then carry on. If the answer is no, then maybe you'll have to make some tough decisions in order to enhance the quality of your life. Does it serve you to be exhausted and exasperated each day? Only you can answer that.

As for the men who believe in traditional gender roles due to religion or other reasons, here's my question for you: is your reason for believing in these roles more important than creating strong relationships and bonds with your children? Again, I can't answer that question for you. What I know for sure is expecting your lady to handle one hundred percent of the childrearing won't build those bonds with your kids, I promise you.

No matter how you slice it, being a good dad requires work, dedication, and sacrifice. If you don't think there are great men in this world who take the art of fatherhood very seriously, you'll definitely want to read about what's coming in the next section.

SECTION 3
DADDIES DOIN' WORK

CHAPTER 14

EMBRACING THE PROCESS

SHATTERED HOOP DREAMS

Rewind to my sophomore year of high school when I was a member of the Junior Varsity basketball team. Our squad just lost a game to our rival school and I played like a steaming pile of hot garbage. Even to this day, I remember the clanking sound of the basketball hitting the rim due to the large amount of free throws I missed, and by the "large amount," I mean all of them. In hindsight, my shooting performance would've made Shaquille O'Neal look like Larry Bird by comparison. As I sat dejected in the locker room, my coach got in my face and told me in no uncertain terms that during the next team workout, he was going to have me practice nothing but free throws while the rest of the team participated in normal drills.

I was one of the best players on the team. Check that—I was THE best player on the team. How dare my coach embarrass me and single me out in front of the whole squad? I was pissed. I sulked. I cursed him under my breath.

That team practice was the longest ninety minutes of my extremely sheltered life.

Once the session ended, my coach pulled me aside and said, "I know you're upset with me right now, but you have to understand something. Being great isn't easy. I've coached so many kids who think that they can just show up and be great, and I'm telling you it just doesn't work that way. You have the potential to be a great player, but I promise that you'll never get there if you don't embrace the process. That means doing the mundane stuff you hate in order to be a well-rounded player, like you did today. Do you understand what I'm saying, son?"

I nodded sheepishly as he smiled and walked away. Once the locker room door shut, I cursed him again for embarrassing me in front of my teammates. That "embrace the process" shit was for the other guys, not for the star of the team.

I wasn't going to change. And why would I? I was already great. It came easy to me.

Clearly, I didn't get it.

When I was finally promoted to the Varsity team the following year, I realized quickly that I was in over my head. The days of dominating five-foot-nine future accountants on the Junior Varsity circuit were over. The players were bigger, stronger, faster, and better than I. Many of my opponents went on to play in college, and I could tell they took their craft seriously. They weren't just great athletes; they also worked extremely hard. Before the games, I'd watch these players practice free throws, passing, dribbling, rebounding, and defense.

Me? Oh, I was the guy practicing dunking. Why? Because that's what the fans like to see. Nobody comes to see a perfect bounce pass. They wanted to see gravity-defying, rim-rocking slam-dunks, and I was the guy to deliver it to them. Not to mention, chicks dig guys who can dunk.

Again, I clearly didn't get it.

My junior and senior years on the Varsity basketball team were littered with extreme disappointment and unrealized potential. I never became the basketball player I expected to be because I never embraced the process of "doin' work" on my game. Don't get me wrong; I wasn't lazy. I just didn't think I had to work in order to be great. "Workin'" was beneath me.

Over twenty years later, I remember the conversation with my JV coach as if he was sitting right next to me now. He had shared one of life's greatest secrets with me and I'd flat out ignored him. Regrets are few and far between in my life, but when I'm alone with my thoughts, I wonder how good I could've been as a player if I embraced the process of doing the mundane tasks I hated. I'll never know, but one thing I know is I would be damned if I don't embrace the process in other areas of my life.

That's the reason why I hate the word "potential." Make no mistake about it, saying someone has potential is just a nice way of saying a person hasn't done it yet, whatever "it" is. Nobody says that Dr. Martin Luther King, Jr. had the potential to be a great orator when he delivered the iconic "I have a dream" speech in Washington, DC. He already was a great orator. I made a decision that if the word potential were thrown my way, the time window to actually *doing it* would be a small one.

Embracing the process isn't just about practicing free throws. It's about being a loyal friend by spending a Saturday to help someone move out of his apartment; it's about being a loving spouse by doing whatever it takes to keep the spark alive; it's about staying physically fit by going to the gym during a snowstorm; and it's about being a good person regardless of how others treat you. Most importantly, it's about doing it *now*. To hell with potential.

IT MUST BE EASY, RIGHT?

Stop me if I've said this before, but being a good dad is not easy.

Okay, so maybe that's not very profound, but no truer words in the realm of *daddyhood* have ever been written. The good news is, there are a lot of men who understand this and put in the requisite work to be the best dads they can be for their families.

Keeping in line with the basketball theme, my favorite athlete was Michael Jordan when I was a teenager. He was tough, talented, charismatic, rich, good-looking, and he was a *winner*. Women wanted to be with him and guys wanted to be him. Hell, Nike created one of the most iconic marketing campaigns of all-time with its "I Want to be Like Mike" ads, because everyone wanted to experience that level of greatness.

To provide you with more background from my earlier story, I desperately wanted to be like Jordan when I was a young basketball player. In my mind, I just figured that if I wished for it hard enough, my life would be just as cool as his. "How hard could it be?" I thought.

Very hard.

The problem is, many people erroneously think it's easy to achieve the status of being a superstar in life. I couldn't secure an interview with Michael Jordan for this book (okay, I didn't try), but if I did, I'm sure he would tell me that none of his success would be possible without putting in the work to be great. Everyone knew his name—and everyone loved him— but it was what he did when nobody was watching that made him a legend.

Going to the weight room early in the morning, jogging

outside in the cold and rain, and taking thousands of practice shots every day is what made him great. So many people have the will to win, but very few have the *will to prepare,* and that's what separates the kings from the clowns.

He embraced the process.

In regards to fatherhood, some men will observe dads who receive public praise from their wives, friends, and kids for being amazing dads, and think, "Hey, I can do that, too." But it's what happens when the outside world isn't looking that makes them special. When they get home from a ridiculously stressful day from work, they change poopy diapers, give baths, read bedtime stories, and seamlessly step into the role of daddy at the blink of an eye. They offer to watch the kids on a random Saturday so their spouses can enjoy a day of relaxation with their friends. When their kids cry for mommy at 3:00 a.m. for the fourth night in a row, they don't wake up their exhausted spouses, but instead, they get up and comfort their babies so their ladies can receive some much-needed rest. No matter what's going on in their lives, they never let their kids or their spouses down. Never.

When dads embrace the process, they do it because they don't want to be average. Stay-at-home dads, single dads, corporate dads, stepdads, etc., it doesn't matter—they want to be great. It's not about their fatigue, their needs, or their stress levels; it's about being the best men they can be for their loved ones. At the end of the day, nothing is more important to them than having families who believe in them, admire them, trust them, and love them.

That's how Daddies Doin' Work are defined.

WHEN THE PROCESS IS NOT EMBRACED

I received the following email from one of my readers named Patricia, and at the time, she was a new mother to a one-month-old baby girl. I'll let her tell the story.

"My husband was so excited to be a father. Since all of his friends have children, he talked a big game about how he would take her to the park, and he boasted that he would happily change diapers, read stories, and give baths. However, once she actually arrived, he became very hands-off. Even though I told him before she was born that it would take a ton of work to be a good dad, he said, 'Oh, I got this. If my friends can do it, so can I.' Now when he comes home from work, he gets upset when I ask him to help out, because he had a busy day and he needs a few hours to unwind before helping out. As if I was just twiddling my thumbs all day or something.

Is he the one who sleeps less than three hours a night? I'm completely exhausted, but he thinks it's perfectly fine to go to happy hour or to the gym after work and leave me alone with the baby every night. Finally, last week I broke down and let him have it. I called him out on not doing anything that he promised. He hasn't taken her on any walks, given her any baths, changed any diapers, or read any stories. He wanted to receive the praise for being a good dad from others, but he wasn't willing to do the work required to be one. To make a [sic] long story short, after a few weeks of arguing, he called me a 'stupid bitch,' moved out, and demanded a divorce.

I am absolutely devastated. A few short weeks ago,

he was so excited to be a father, but now that the baby is actually here, he turned into someone I hardly recognize."

Nobody is ever truly ready to become a parent because the job is so incredibly unpredictable. No two days are alike, and no two kids are alike (even my identical twin and I aren't completely alike). But similar to superstar athletes, popular musicians, doctors, teachers, etc., the cream of the crop knows how difficult it is to be great and they take part in the mundane tasks in order to reach greatness.

Let's keep it real for a moment; there's nothing cool about waking up at 3:00 a.m. to calm a crying baby. There's nothing cool about changing crap-filled diapers so fragrant that they singe nose hairs. There's nothing cool about getting spit up on or thrown up on. And there's nothing cool about doing any of this after enduring a long day at work.

Not only are these tasks *not* cool, they also categorically suck. But these dads do it anyway, because they embrace the process of being great dads. The payoff is a bond created with his children that a jackhammer couldn't separate.

And is there anything more important than creating a bond with our children? For Daddies Doin' Work, there isn't.

CHAPTER 15
THE LESSONS OF A DADDY DOIN' WORK

FAKE TOUGHNESS V. REAL TOUGHNESS

Just like many high schools across America, mine was littered with bullies and more often than not, I got my ass handed to me verbally or physically by them. These kids yelled a lot, they got into fights, and they rarely showed any sensitive emotions (at least not publicly, like I did). So, I'd often hear the word "tough" being thrown around when I was around them, but I never understood why. In their world, it seemed as if being tough was synonymous with being an asshole. Is being a man all about demonstrating dominance over another person? In my heart I knew better, but I didn't know what to do about it.

When I finally talked to my parents about what toughness entails, my dad offered the following thoughts: "Being tough is not about being violent, being loud, or being mean-spirited. That's fake toughness. Real men are mentally and emotionally strong, aren't afraid to be vulnerable, and always do the right thing even when others may ridicule them."

It took a while for it to sink in, but my dad was absolutely right. When I was growing up, it was rare to hear the words, "vulnerable," "sensitive," "caring," and "loving" on the list of qualities dads demonstrated or wanted for their kids (especially their sons), but the tide is turning. Daddies Doin' Work not only embrace the mundane tasks of fatherhood, they smash stereotypes in regard to what being a good dad is all about in the modern world. It would be damn near impossible to list every possible parenting trick these men use, so we'll touch on the main themes here. If you're involved with a Daddy Doin' Work, a lot of what you're about to read will be very familiar to you.

HIS JOB IS WHAT HE DOES, NOT WHO HE IS

A friend of mine is a corporate guy, and he's recognized as a superstar at his job by his peers, clients, and superiors. Recently, he was offered a promotion to become the senior manager of his department, and with that title comes a hefty thirty-eight-thousand-dollar raise and the luxury of finally moving out of the cubicle farm into his very own office. With a door. A door that he could close whenever he wanted to escape his crazy coworkers. Man, he really wanted that door.

He's also a happily married dad with two young children, and as much as that extra money would assist his family—and that office door would assist his mental welfare—he turned the promotion down. Many of his peers thought he was crazy. Some of the senior leaders thought he couldn't handle the pressures of management. He knew better.

He knew the role would entail late nights spent in the office, business trips taken multiple times a month, and being on call practically twenty-four seven. Without hesitation, he decided the promotion was not worth the extra money and perks. What's the significance of some extra cash and a glass door if they take time away from the people he loved most? He's smart enough to know that time with his family is his most valuable resource, and he wasn't willing to give it up.

When I talked to him about his decision, he smiled as if he's answered the question for the hundredth time,

> *"This job is what I do, it's not who I am. I'm a dad and a husband first. Yes, I love that my current job provides me with a solid income and great benefits, but the promotion would cut into the asset I value the most, and that's time with my family. My kids are growing so fast, and I don't want to miss any more moments than I need to. Some may view me as being irresponsible for not taking more money, but I think it would be irresponsible for me if I did."*

That's not to say corporate leaders, doctors, lawyers, or entrepreneurs can't be Daddies Doin' Work, because many of them are. It's just that what they do for a living never becomes more important than being a dad. If their jobs require them to be away from their families for long periods of time, you can bet your ass that they are actively involved with their kids and spouses as soon as they arrive home.

The reason why my friend is a superstar at his job is because when he's there, he's there to work. He doesn't spend time messing around on the Internet, he doesn't take extended lunch breaks, and he is a hard working employee when he's "between the lines." He does it because he knows that if he busts his ass while he's at work, he'll never have to spend a minute in the office longer than he needs to when the day ends. In other words, he's a fully-engaged superstar at work so he can be a fully-engaged superstar at home.

SHOWING UP

Daddies Doin' Work always show up. And by "showing up," I mean they are always there either physically, emotionally, or spiritually for their children. Whenever it's possible for them to do so, they'll show up to their son's baseball game or their daughter's dance recital. They step away from a work-related meeting to help solve a crisis for their kids who are away at college. Even if they're deployed overseas for the military, they'll take what little available time they have to video conference with their families or send emails. Put simply, they are always there.

Too many children are left disappointed when it comes to their dads just not showing up. As we know, the Daddies Doin' Nothing don't show up for anything (birthdays, sporting events, dance recitals, etc.). Daddies Doin' Something show up only when it's convenient for them (after a meeting, when the big game is over, after they're done relaxing after a long day at the office, etc.).

What separates a Daddy Doin' Work from the rest is that he does work for his kids even when it's inconvenient for him. It could be a simple hug from his toddler son, helping his teenage daughter with homework, teaching his son how to properly throw a curveball, or being a shoulder to cry on when his daughter gets her heart broken by a boy.

Few things are more important to children than knowing their dads will always be there for them. My parents always told me that the people who matter in my life will always show up. And they always have.

YOU WANT CREDIT FOR . . . WHAT?

A few years ago at my corporate job, a customer service trainer approached me, and he was livid because he received a "Meets Expectations" rating on his annual performance review. He vented to me for about ten minutes in a fit of rage.

"How could they give me a 'Meets Expectations' rating? I busted my ass for this company! I deserve an 'Outstanding' rating for all of the work I put in for them! I'm so tired of this shit!"

When I asked him what he did to deserve an Outstanding rating, he complained about how he gave one hundred percent effort, showed up to work on time, and trained a certain amount of classes during the calendar year.

That's when I countered by asking, "Well, isn't that what you're supposed to do? It's in your job description, right?" At that point, he mumbled some obscenities and walked away. Who knows if he actually realized it, but he wanted credit for doing the work he was hired to do: give one hundred percent effort, show up to work on time, and train the requisite amount of classes during a calendar year. He did those things; but he wanted to be treated like a king because of it.

It's the same in the daddy realm as well. There are some guys who think they should receive an "Outstanding" review for doing what's in their job description as dads. Daddies Doin' Work don't look for praise and back-patting for changing diapers, cooking dinner, reading bedtime stories, or waking up in the middle of the night to comfort a crying baby. As a matter of fact, they'll be the first to deflect praise when it's given to them because they understand that it's all a part of the being a dad. In other words, they're meeting the expectations of the job description.

Logically they understand that most moms do these things every day for their children and nobody is telling them how awesome they are. So why should they expect anything different in return? For them, it's not about praise. It's about being involved, it's about caring, and it's about being a real man.

Of course, these great men like to receive credit for going above and beyond the call of duty (who doesn't?), but what my former co-worker didn't know is that in order to receive an "Outstanding" performance review, he has to do outstanding shit. In no universe does showing up to work on time and giving one hundred percent effort qualify as outstanding. Every company expects such from every employee, just like every woman should expect her man to complete normal parenting tasks.

These men set the bar extremely high, and their families are the beneficiaries. No, it's not easy, but as mentioned earlier, if it were easy, everyone would be doin' work, right?

ENOUGH OF THE GENDER STEREOTYPES

When Emiko was two and a half years old, I asked her what she wanted to be for Halloween. Since my daughter was like most two-and-a-half-year-olds, she usually had no idea what she wanted unless it involved food; then the answer is always Graham Crackers. But she surprised me when she looked up at me and said, "I wanna be Spider-Man, Daddy."

Wait, come again? You want to be Spider-Man? Peter Parker's alter ego? The guy who was bitten by a radioactive spider and has super agility, super strength, and can climb walls? Is that the person she wanted to be for Halloween? My immediate reaction was, "Absolutely, you can be Spider-Man for Halloween!" For some reason, she had an infatuation with one of the world's most popular superheroes, and I wasn't about to deny her from dressing up as him.

When I told some of my friends about it, I received a few stink eyes. They were like, "Really, Doyin? You're going to dress up your baby girl as a male superhero? What's wrong with dressing her up as a princess or Dora the Explorer instead?" Nothing at all. But I operate with the mentality that my girls can be whatever they want to be. Superheroes? Sure. Firefighters? Absolutely. Army Rangers? Cool with me. I never want to limit my daughters' imagination by pigeonholing them into something that they may not be into. Most Daddies Doin' Work are the same way. They are always building up their kids by giving them the confidence to be whatever their little hearts desire.

Now here's where it gets tricky: most dads probably wouldn't riot if their daughters wanted to dress up as Spider-Man for Halloween. But what if their sons wanted to play with dolls? A Daddy Doin' Work I interviewed, named Rick, shares his story:

> "My son is four years old and he enjoys playing with dolls and putting on his big sister's princess dresses. My wife thinks it's cute, and I have no issues with it whatsoever; but if you surveyed my friends and extended family, they would have a completely different opinion. I've been called everything from a deadbeat to a queer-lover and everything in between. Most of them think that, as a father, I should steer my son toward more 'manly' activities like playing with monster trucks and action figures instead of making his life 'more difficult in the future by allowing him to act like a girl.'
>
> "My role as a dad is not to teach him what is stereotypically expected of boys. My role is to teach him to be

mentally strong, confident, and sure of himself. Playing with dolls has nothing to do with that goal. As long as he's safe and happy, he can do whatever his little heart desires. And guess what? He's safe and he's very happy. I will never force my kids to be something that they're not."

Rick employs a very progressive viewpoint, and there are some dads out there who probably wouldn't let their sons dress up as princesses or let their daughters dress up as male superheroes. My belief is that a kid's sexuality isn't going to be determined by whether he or she finds interest in toys or games that traditionally interest kids of the opposite sex; and if it did, so what? Would we stop loving them because of it? Again, I'm not going to get into a discussion about religion and sexuality, but I will say this: if we stop our children from doing what they want to do (assuming they're safe and happy, of course), it won't change anything. They will always find a way to express who they really are whether we like it or not. So why not let them explore life and make decisions for themselves?

OWN YOUR BOMBNESS

Daddies Doin' Work are very confident in their "daddying" abilities. They're not perfect—no parent is—but they wake up every day knowing that their kids' lives are better because of the love, support, and influence they provide them. In other words, they own their bombness. To be clear, you don't have to be an egotistical douchebag to own your bombness. Owning your bombness also isn't walking around saying, "Hey everybody! Check out how great I am!" As a matter of fact, it's the complete opposite. If you're really good at something, you never have to say a word about it. People will *just know*.

When a Daddy Doin' Work raises his kids, he does his part to ensure his kids own their bombness, too. It's a simple concept: if someone compliments his kids, he wants them to own it. It's not about saying, "Thanks, but . . ." or offering contrary evidence. He teaches his kids to own that shit.

For example, when someone compliments them for being funny, they are taught to own it. We all know how many un-funny people there are in the world. We also know how much it sucks to be around them, but can you imagine how much it sucks to actually *be* them? Luckily, it's not a problem for these kids.

Teaching kids to own their bombness in all aspects of life gives them the ammunition to deal with the bullies and haters they'll inevitably encounter as they get older. A single Daddy Doin' Work, named Dan, shares a powerful story on how it worked for him and his daughters:

> *"I'm a single dad, and in my personal experience I see a lot of parents spending their time telling kids what they can't do. Stupid shit like telling them not to use the monkey bars at the playground fearing they'll fall. Newsflash to all of those parents: YES, your kid will fall! And there's a good chance they'll hurt themselves when they fall. Then the magic happens. When you comfort kids and tell them that sometimes in life these things happen and to try again, they feel empowered, not scared. Kids are messy, they're dirty, they're clumsy, and they're awkward, but all of that is beautiful. All they're trying to do is figure out their way in the world, and as a dad my goal is to guide them and not be a dictator. It doesn't matter if it's math, the way they look, or anything in between; I always build up their confidence and never offer any words that will*

crush their spirits. Not a day passes when I don't tell my girls that they're smart, beautiful, funny, and just plain awesome. In doing so, they have the attitude that they can conquer the world."

I also see dads who think fear is the best way to raise their kids. These poor children are constantly looking over their shoulders, afraid to death to mess up, because they know that a tongue-lashing or a smack in the face will surely follow. That never made any sense to me. Why would any dad want his kids to be scared of him? How does that positively affect their confidence and self-esteem? In my opinion, any dad who uses aggressive behavior to raise his kids probably doesn't have the emotional maturity or intelligence to be a dad in the first place.

"My daughters are eleven and fourteen now, and both of them get bullied in school. The cool thing is that both of them are so confident that they brush it off by saying, 'Wow, I can't believe someone is crazy enough not to see how cool and nice I am. It must really suck for them.' Some people may think that's an egotistical way to approach life, but what's better? Being a slave to the words and actions of bullies and haters? Growing up thinking that disrespectful men are all they deserve to marry? Constantly worrying that their body types aren't what society 'demands' of them? Also, when they fail, they aren't devastated by it. Instead, they dust themselves off and go back after it with intensified vigor. Being the first man my daughters ever loved, it's my responsibility to constantly tell them how great they are; and I believe that my philosophy helped them become the strong and happy young women they are today."

In other words, Dan teaches his girls to own their bomb-ness, and now they're living a charmed life. For kids to consistently hear how amazing they are from their daddies, their superheroes, goes so incredibly far.

NICE PEOPLE ALWAYS FINISH FIRST

Having smart and attractive kids is great and all, but it's meaningless unless they have good hearts and care about other people beside themselves. Daddies Doin' Work teach their kids to never be bullies, make fun of people, or be mean-spirited jack-asses. Tony, a Daddy Doin' Work living in San Diego, shares his story:

> *"I have two boys, and above all else I teach them to be gentlemen. That means respecting women, always saying please and thank you, holding doors open for people, looking people in the eye during conversation, and putting the needs of others before their own. I've seen dads that are so wrapped up in their day jobs and other foolishness that they don't even notice when their sons become emotionally unavailable zombies and their daughters become snarky mean girls.*
>
> *"Being involved as a dad means teaching my boys to display empathy for others. If they see the so-called class nerd sitting by herself at lunchtime, they'll offer to sit with her. If someone is getting bullied at school, they'll stand up for him. In a nutshell, they just care, and that's why I'm so proud of them. The world is changing now. Most dads aren't teaching the antiquated rhetoric to their kids that nice people finish last. That's bullshit. You can have all of the looks, money, and talent in the world, but none of it*

matters if you're not a nice person. I think it was Maya Angelou who said, 'People may not remember exactly what you did, or what you said, but they will always remember how you made them feel.'"

Seems simple, right? I always tell people that if everyone made the effort to smile at least to one stranger a day, the world would become an infinitely happier place. A freaking smile, flexing your mouth muscles for two whole seconds, would change the way the world behaves in a positive way. I digress, but Daddies Doin' Work understand that being kind and teaching kindness to their children is more important than trying to be heavy-handed tough guys.

DADDY AFFECTION

Daddies Doin' Work are always affectionate, and they have their own ways of expressing it to their children. It could be a hug or kiss, it could a tickle fight, it could be an impromptu dance party, it could be a tag-team effort to complete a difficult puzzle, it could be telling his kids how much he loves them, it could be leaving post-it notes in his kids' lunchboxes while he's away on a business trip, or it could be anything that shows his children how much he cares about them.

Most of the dads I know do this stuff on a daily basis, but there are some I've seen who never give hugs, never utter an "I love you," and rarely offer any physical contact unless it's an ass-whooping to their kids when they "get out of line." Those are the same dads who will give their kids money on their birthdays and think that they're the world's greatest dads because of it.

Tony, the Daddy Doin' Work in the previous segment,

quoted Maya Angelou, and those words are extremely powerful. People will always remember how you make them *feel*.
Even today, I can think back to some extremely fond memories
I experienced with my parents from when I was very young.
For example, I remember the thrill I felt when my dad told
me how proud he was when I received an "A++" on a paper I
wrote for my sixth grade Social Studies class. Shit, I can't even
remember what the topic of the paper was, but I sure remember how I *felt* when he hugged me and said how happy he was
for me. That stuff matters, and Daddies Doin' Work get that.
It doesn't matter if they spent twelve hours getting their asses
chewed out by their bosses; when they get home, they always
make time for their children by demonstrating that nothing in
life is more important than their family. Nothing.

Reginald, a Daddy Doin' Work living in Michigan, gives
an example of how important displaying affection is to him:

> *"When I'm around my son and daughter, I don't think
> an hour passes when I don't hug them, kiss them, and
> tell them how much I love them. I work as a software
> engineer, and my days are pretty long, but no day is long
> enough for me not to have time to show affection to my
> children. Why even bother having children if you aren't
> willing to shower them with love and affection? Since
> they're both very young, I'm not sure what problems my
> kids will encounter when they get older, but I can promise
> you that none of those problems will be due to a lack of
> love and affection they receive from their daddy."*

THE END RESULT

To put it all together, dads who teach their kids to be who they are, love themselves, be kind to others—while offering affection in the process—will increase the likelihood of raising happy, healthy, successful children. As Frederick Douglass once said, "It's easier to build strong children than to repair broken men." Of course, there are a lot of moms who teach these lessons already, but what good does it do if those lessons are offset by crappy or mediocre dads who just don't get it?

If your man is a Daddy Doin' Work, all of what you just read will be familiar to you, because he gets it. And the best part is that you and your children are the beneficiaries of his awesomeness. Of course, a few women reading this will think, "Damn, my man doesn't do any of this," which undoubtedly means he's planted in the Daddy Doin' Nothing or Daddy Doin' Something category.

If you happen to be an unhappy mom due to the type of guy you had children with, I hope you now know that there are men in this world who do the right thing for their families. A lot of men. Every dad I'm friends with behaves this way or else we wouldn't be friends. Don't succumb to the noise that every man is a selfish, lazy piece of garbage. We aren't. At the end of the day, you need to determine if you want to suffer in silence or if you want to take action and make a better life for you and your kids. Have him read this chapter, discuss your feelings with him, show him that there are men who do more than bring home a paycheck; and flat out ask him if he feels if he's offering enough to your family emotionally.

What is the worst thing that can happen? If he gets mad, it's because you flashed a mirror in his face and asked him to determine what kind of a dad he is. If he doesn't like what he sees, he's going to direct his anger at you. If he threatens to leave, let him. Good luck finding a woman like you who does everything around the house. Your kids will be better off for it. If he calls you ungrateful due to you not recognizing all he does for the family (aka, bringing home a paycheck), then ask him how that money helps to foster a relationship with his children. Does Benjamin Franklin hop off of a hundred dollar bill to comfort your son when he's upset or play dress up with your daughter? Sure, money provides shelter, food, and clothing, but it doesn't provide love. There are millions of Daddies Doin' Work who bust their asses at their jobs and still come home to transform into loving, attentive daddies. Why can't he?

The best part? The Daddies Doin' Work of the world don't think they're Super Dads. They are simply doing what comes naturally to them. Everything described in this chapter is as natural to them as breathing. No woman should settle for anything less.

CHAPTER 16

ARE YOU INVOLVED WITH A DADDY DOIN' WORK? KEEP IT THAT WAY

WE DESCRIBED WHAT DADDIES DOIN' Work are all about, and if you're involved with one, you should rejoice. He's hard working, kind, caring, and is intrinsically motivated to step up for your family in any way possible. Oftentimes, these men won't need any assistance to continue exhibiting their status as amazing daddies. But here's what you and the rest of the world need to ensure he stays on-track.

BACK THE HELL UP AND LET HIM DO HIS THING

The most daunting enemies of Daddies Doin' Work all over the world are micromanaging moms who nitpick them for everything. Men and women are different; while I can't understand how some women find it enjoyable to curl up on the couch to cry while watching a sappy love story, I'm sure some women can't understand how some men find it enjoyable to obsess over the movements of adult men in tight pants on football fields across America every autumn Sunday (guilty as charged).

Men and women do almost everything differently, so it's to

be expected that he may tackle parenting tasks a little differently than you do. And that's okay. He may allow your daughter to munch on more junk food than you would normally allow; he may put your son into an outfit that doesn't perfectly match; he may allow his daughter to take more risks at the playground; and he may be the world's worst hairstylist. But at the end of the day, does any of that matter? If he's focused on being the best dad he can be for his children, back the hell up and let him do his thing.

Here's the big difference between the two versions of daddies (not including the Daddies Doin' Nothing): micromanaging a Daddy Doin' Something for how he does his job as a dad will make him back off completely while his female partner is stuck doing everything. When the same happens to a Daddy Doin' Work, he may harbor a healthy amount of resentment towards his spouse or may end up walking away from the relationship completely.

Bryan, a Daddy Doin' Work in Texas, is a perfect example. I'll let him tell his story:

> "I dated my longtime girlfriend for eight years before we decided to have our son Sean. I love my son very much and I happily change diapers, go to the park, read bedtime stories, or wake up in the middle of the night to comfort him if needed. Overall, I embrace everything that fatherhood throws at me with open arms. The problem is that my now ex-girlfriend took away the joy from me.
>
> "Nothing was ever good enough for her. If I gave my son a bath, she would comment on how I did it wrong, she would laugh whenever I attempted to cook dinner for the family, and she micromanaged anything I did that involved my son. It got to the point where she wouldn't

leave me alone with Sean for fear that I'd somehow 'break him.' After six months of it, I decided that we needed to seek counseling because I was tired of second guessing myself every time I interacted with my child. During our first counseling session, my ex stated, 'No man can do a better job parenting than a woman can. It's just a fact. We nurtured our babies for nine months in the womb and we know them before they even enter the world. I'm sorry, but he just doesn't do things as well as I can, and I let him know about it. Maybe he shouldn't be so sensitive. I'm sure every mother acts that way.'

"*At that point, I knew our relationship was doomed. I love Sean. He's a wonderful little boy, but I knew that I wouldn't be the dad he deserved if I stayed in a soul crushing relationship that drained my energy. It's patently false that men can't parent as well as women, just like it's patently false that every woman acts the way my ex does. And after three months of counseling, we decided to go our separate ways.*

"*Currently, I'm in a happy marriage with my new wife, Amanda, and I'm an even better father to Sean without constantly looking over my shoulder. We have our different philosophies in regards to how we raise children, but the end result is always that if our kids are happy and healthy, nothing else really matters.*

"*If I could offer any advice to your female readers, it would be to be careful not to discourage the good dads of the world who genuinely care about being helpful. A few weeks ago my ex admitted to me that her biggest regret was pushing me away, but it's too late now.*"

NOTE: Brian now has a daughter with his wife.

Bryan's advice is solid. Unfortunately, there are women who take pleasure in poking fun at their men for how they raise their kids, but when that happens to a guy who takes fatherhood as seriously as Daddies Doin' Work do, it could end badly for these ladies and their relationships. This cannot be stressed enough: if your man is a Daddy Doin' Work, you need to be careful on how and when you deliver critiques to him. Being a good dad means the world to him and because of that, he wants to learn in order to do the best job he can. If he's addressed respectfully when feedback is offered instead of being treated like a moron, he'll probably take it to heart and appreciate it.

Also, it's important to determine if some battles are worth fighting. If he's checking football scores on his phone while your toddler daughter starts swinging around the scissors he left on the kitchen table, that's absolutely worth addressing. However, if he puts your son in a brown shirt instead of the blue one you prefer, is it worth raising a stink over to potentially demoralize him? Just take a deep breath and let him express his "daddyness." Tomorrow you won't even remember it. He's not perfect and he'll make mistakes, but damn—that guy loves his kids. The world needs more men like him, not less.

APPRECIATION V. PRAISE

Daddies Doin' Work aren't doin' daily daddyhood duties (say that five times fast) in order to receive praise for how great they are. As a matter of fact, they are the first ones to roll their eyes or scratch their heads whenever someone offers them props for taking their kids to the park or changing their diapers. They understand that dads are *supposed* to do these things as a part of their job descriptions, and offering praise to people for doing what they're supposed to do is making the ordinary become extraordinary. In other words, it's no different than giving an employee praise for showing up to work on time. Nothing good comes from that nonsense.

However, don't mistake praising a man for his work. We all want to be appreciated for a job well done, right? For example, many SAHMs view their jobs as the most unappreciated on the planet, and if you happen to be a SAHM, you understand how tough it is to bust your ass every day and not have anyone give you a pat on the back for your efforts. You don't want a parade or people to say how amazing you are. You just want to know that the people you care for daily appreciate what you do for them. Simple as that.

It's no different for Daddies Doin' Work. Part of being in the club is appreciating the women they had children with (assuming they are still happily involved with them). And ladies, please be sure you return the favor as well.

Our friend Brian is back to talk about this dynamic.

"What makes Amanda (his wife) so special is that she always lets me know how much she appreciates me and not the tasks I complete. She doesn't thank me for changing diapers, brushing our kids' hair, or giving them baths everyday, and quite frankly, I don't want her to; but she always lets me know in verbal and non-verbal ways how much I mean to her. It could be a hug, a kiss, a surprise dinner date, or a sincere 'I love you.' It doesn't take much, but those small acts of appreciation from the woman I chose to spend the rest of my life with makes it

so I would run through a brick wall for my family. Words cannot express how much that means to me."

If you're one of the lucky ones who happen to be married to a Daddy Doin' Work, he will always demonstrate how much he appreciates you through thoughtful acts. Be sure to keep showing him how much you appreciate the work he puts in for your families as well. You know what makes him happy, so continue to do those things for him. It doesn't really matter what it is as long as it's done consistently.

BUILD YOUR RELATIONSHIP

Any woman in love with a Daddy Doin' Work will tell you that it's way more positive than negative. But there are times when these men will be so focused on their love for their children that they put the love they have for their spouses on the backburner. You wouldn't have to look very far to find men complaining about the lack of passion with their spouses once babies entered the picture, but it happens to some women, too.

If you were like me as a kid, you probably loved to run up the "down" escalators at your local shopping mall because it required twice as much effort to make it to the top. That's exactly what a relationship is like when children are in the picture. We have to work twice as hard to ensure our kids and spouses are happy. If we put in the same effort as we did before babies came around (using this analogy, it would mean walking up the down escalator), we wouldn't get anywhere. Even though it can be damn exhausting at times, you have to keep running.

When a man puts in the amount of work that a Daddy Doin' Work does on a daily basis, it's not surprising when he's completely wiped out when his kids are in bed for the night. And when it's time for him to go to bed with his spouse, the "S" word on his mind usually is sleep, not sex. As an actively involved mom yourself, no one would fault you for choosing to stare at your eyelids over playing "hide the salami" as your late night activity of choice. But it's more than physical passion.

Here's the positive part: in the history of the universe no child has suffered developmentally due to two parents loving each other. Play hooky from work and send the kids to day-care while you and your man enjoy a childless day together. Find a babysitter and have a regular date night. Don't let the "Mommy? Mommy! MOMMY!" banter interrupt a hug or kiss that you're giving your man. The kids will be okay, I promise.

As you're reading these words, somewhere there's a flight attendant telling his passengers that in the event of an emergency the adults should put their oxygen masks on prior to doing so for their children. Before I had kids, I always thought that was strange. I mean, wouldn't it make more sense for parents to take care of their kids before themselves? All I heard growing up is how the best parents are extremely unselfish, but what's more selfish than that?

Now that I'm a parent, I totally understand. It's impossible to be the best mom or dad you can be without taking care of yourself and your partner.

PATERNITY LEAVE

There are some societal issues that make the lives of great dads more difficult than necessary. Currently, the United States is the last industrialized country that doesn't have a law mandating that new moms receive a certain amount of paid days off from their employers due to the birth of a baby; so, it doesn't take a genius to figure out that there's no law for dads, either. Yes, because of the Family Medical Leave Act (FMLA), qualified parents of newborn babies are allowed twelve weeks of leave that guarantees their jobs will be safe upon their return. The bad news is, employers have zero obligations to pay their employees while they're away from work.

When you step back and realize how back-asswards it is for the great U.S. of A to wallow behind pretty much the entire free world when it comes to baby bonding, it will make your head spin. And whenever I take a look at the amazing baby bonding benefits other countries enjoy it's no secret why the rest of the world laughs at us.

Daddies Doin' Work have to deal with a lot when it comes to taking time off from their careers to bond with a newborn baby, and getting paid (or not getting paid) is usually at the top of the list. If he provides the only income for his family, do you think he can possibly take three months off to bond with a child if the paychecks stop coming in? Probably not. In some cases, his family may not be able to survive financially if he takes *three days* off from work to bond with a child, and that's a damn shame.

But what if he works for one of those rare American companies that offers paid baby bonding leave? It would be a no-brainer for a Daddy Doin' Work to jump all over that, right? Well, not so fast. At the end of the day, the great dads of the world don't hesitate to take a paid paternity leave from their jobs, but they won't be faulted if there's a nagging feeling in the back of their minds while they're home. They may worry that their reputations in the office will be damaged by leaving their teams "high and dry" to pick up their workloads. They may wonder if other jealous colleagues are conspiring behind their backs while they're away. They may believe that the big wigs in the office will view them as unreliable employees due to their "lack of commitment" to the company. It's not paranoia. Please know that somewhere in this country, there's a Daddy Doin' Work dealing with this *right now*.

Ethan, a first-time dad, tells his paternity leave story:

"When I worked in advertising for a large company, I remember how excited I was when I learned that my wife was pregnant with our first child. Luckily my employer has a policy in place to pay a portion of my salary if I decided to take baby bonding leave, so without even thinking about it, I signed up for it. When I approached my male boss about taking four weeks off when my baby was born, I could tell that he was less than thrilled. To prevent himself from getting in trouble with human resources, he knew better than to say something stupid to my face, so he resorted to other passive aggressive tactics. During a team meeting a few weeks later, he smugly said, 'In my entire professional career I've never taken a vacation longer than a week. Wanna know why? Because if a company can survive without me being there for longer than a week, then it probably means that I don't add much value and they could get rid of me at a moment's notice. But hey, to each his own.' Even some of my team members (male and female) gave me grief for taking 'so much time off.' They thought it was a woman's job to do that, not the dad's. I wish I could say that these people were isolated to my company, but unfortunately, this foolishness is common in workplaces all over the country. Why not celebrate men who choose to bond with their kids? Who

in their right minds are more committed to their jobs than their families? I just don't get it."

Ladies, I'm not saying you are immune to the same workplace tomfoolery, but it's a completely different ballgame for you. Most reasonable people believe that a mom *needs* to be at home for a newborn, oftentimes due to the fact that she is the sole source of the baby's food supply. The problem stems from society not believing that the dad *needs* to be there, too. America just views his involvement with a newborn to be a luxury and we really need to take a moment and ask ourselves why.

Can dads feed babies, too? Sure they can as long as the mom chooses to express breast milk into a bottle or if the family uses formula instead.

Can dads soothe, nurture, and comfort babies? Of course, they can.

Can dads bathe babies, change diapers, get babies dressed, and rock them to sleep? Of course, they can.

Outside of breastfeeding, what can a mom do that a dad can't? Absolutely nothing.

So then why does America and the overwhelming majority of American companies view a dad's involvement with a newborn to be a luxury instead of a necessity? Why should a man who actively wants to bond with his baby be denied from doing so because he can't afford it? Why should a man fear that there will be retaliation from his employer if he takes paid time off to be with his newborn just because they operate under the belief that it's a woman's responsibility? I don't have the answers to these questions, but that doesn't relinquish the power from us to make a change.

We can write to our elected officials, speak up at town hall meetings, send a note to the senior leaders of corporations, create a community outreach groups, start social media pages dedicated to paternity leave; but no matter what it is, we have to do something to raise awareness and build momentum. It's not like mandated baby bonding leave is such a ground-breaking concept. If it was, why are countless other countries onboard with it except for the land of the free and the home of the brave? For the sake of future generations of dads and moms (a.k.a. our children) we cannot allow this to continue any longer.

TIME FOR A (DIAPER) CHANGE

Paternity leave is a huge obstacle for dads, but there's another issue that doesn't receive nearly the amount of publicity but is equally as demoralizing.

Recently, my wife and Emiko spent some "girl time" together on a Saturday afternoon, so I took Reiko out on the town. During our excursion, she made that unmistakable "baby poop face" and I knew she left a big present for Daddy to clean up.

I took her to the men's restroom of an unnamed establishment and there was no changing table. What about a family restroom? Nope, there wasn't one. Then I noticed that the women's restroom door was propped open due to it being cleaned and there was a changing table in plain sight.

So what did I do?

This time, I quietly left and changed her in the back of my SUV without raising a fuss. As I typed a lengthy email to the corporate offices, I realized that this is a huge problem. Companies like this are basically saying, *"Only women can change diapers here."* This is not okay.

First, let's be clear about who the enemy is. There are plenty of establishments that have changing tables in *both* restrooms or have family restrooms. Obviously they're our friends.

There are establishments that don't have changing tables in *any* of their restrooms, which basically sends the message that they don't cater to young children. As a parent with two young children, I'm totally cool with this. If they don't want my kids in their place of business, I'll either go there without my kids or they won't get my hard-earned cash. I'm not a parent who thinks every establishment should be kid-friendly. Quite honestly, there are some places I enjoy going to simply because they *don't* cater to children.

The source of my ire is solely directed upon the businesses that consciously decide to install changing tables in women's restrooms, but not in the men's restrooms (and have no family restrooms, either). They're fine with young children visiting their establishments, but if they soil themselves, there better be a woman around to take care of it. Do you know what's scary? Many of these businesses weren't built in the 1950s; actually, many are brand-spanking new. I can just picture what the owners must have thought when they made that decision.

"Only chicks change diapers, so we're not going to waste time putting a changing table in the men's room. Only a punk-ass man would complain about not being able to change a diaper here, anyway."

I ain't no punk-ass man, and neither are the men who believe in sharing parenting responsibilities with their partners.

It's unbelievably sexist against men and women to operate this way. What about single dads? What about gay dads? What if a dad was out by himself and it was freezing cold, raining, or snowing outside and he had to change his baby in the backseat of his car? What if a dad felt that the best option was to change his precious baby on the grimy floor of a public restroom? Ladies, I'm sure many of you had your stomach turn at the thought of that, but you'd be shocked to know how many times I've witnessed this happen in my lifetime.

The "changing table problem" isn't helping the effort to create a world of more good, involved dads. There are a sizable percentage of men, when faced with the no-changing-table-in-the-men's-restroom dilemma, who would simply throw up their hands and walk back to their spouses with their smelly kids in tow saying, "It looks like you'll have to change little Johnny. Hey, it's not my fault! There's no changing table in there!" or even worse, have the kids suffer in a soiled diaper until they get home if their spouses aren't with them.

Being about as subtle as a sledgehammer, society drops another horrible example of how far we need to go to level the playing field when it comes to parental responsibilities. There are plenty of Daddies Doin' Work out there who share my outrage about this, but on the flip side, there are also some knuckleheaded dads who use these examples as *proof* that they shouldn't be taking care of these diaper-changing duties in the first place. That's a problem.

Business owners will need to decide if it's worth pissing off millions of great dads by not having changing tables in *both* restrooms. What about the frustrated moms reading this? I know they're not happy about this either. No one in his right mind wants to anger you ladies.

Final memo to companies all over the world: nobody is asking you to explain the Higgs boson to us. We only want a changing table in your men's restroom if you already have one in your women's restroom, or at the very least a family restroom. Again, if you decide that you're not a kid-friendly establishment and refuse to install any changing tables in your men's or women's restrooms, that's totally fine by me, and you'll be labeled as such. If you have a family restroom instead of a changing table in the men's restroom, that's a good start, but why not just finish the job by installing one in all of your restrooms?

If you operate a company, business, or restaurant that's doing the right thing—namely, it has changing tables in the men's and women's restrooms—you will be celebrated. Sure, it seems like a strange thing to celebrate, but until it becomes commonplace, it's important to give props to the ones who embrace the simple fact that dads change diapers, too.

If you operate a company, business, or restaurant with a changing table in the women's restroom but not in the men's restroom (and there's no family restroom available), don't be surprised if you see dads changing diapers in places where you don't want them to, like a dining room table in your restaurants or in your women's restrooms. Also, don't be surprised to see patrons complaining to the manager/business owner about operating in the time warp you're stuck in. And most importantly, don't be surprised when customers stop giving you their money altogether.

In the interest of full disclosure, I have no experience when it comes to installing a changing table in a restroom, but I'm fairly confident that it isn't complicated or expensive to do. And even if it is complicated or expensive to do, is that one-time experience more daunting than losing potential customers, receiving horrible press, and dealing with drama from unhappy patrons? No way. In this day and age, it's completely inexcusable.

We can do better, America. And now is the time.

IF YOU'RE LUCKY, STAY LUCKY

Some of you reading this chapter may think, "Dude, I already know all of this." Good for you. But if I had a dollar for every woman I've come across who acted as if she had all of the answers to keeping her amazing man happy, but ended up failing miserably, I'd buy a private jet and fly to their houses to share all of the stories in person. As mentioned earlier, I receive countless emails from great dads who complain about their wives or girlfriends who have no clue on how to treat them. Don't be that lady.

None of this is intended to be profound. It's no different than the college kid who knows if he studies for his Chemistry exam, he'll most likely receive a better grade than if he spends the days leading up to the exam getting drunk at fraternity parties. So, if he knows this, why is he running around in his boxer shorts doing keg stands? The person who says, "Knowledge is power" has no idea what he's talking about. Knowledge doesn't mean shit if it's not used properly.

Always remember these tips when interacting with your Daddy Doin' Work. He has the hard part covered, namely, being a positive role model to your children and being a great partner to you; however, just be aware of the pitfalls that could get in the way and negatively impact your relationship.

CHAPTER 17

COGNITIVE DISSONANCE: THE UNIQUE PLIGHT OF AFRICAN-AMERICAN DADS

Now that we know traits a Daddy Doin' Work demonstrates and the issues they encounter in a general sense, the next few chapters will dive deeper into a few types of these great men, their challenges, and what makes them special.

THE ERRONEOUS PERCEPTION

We made it all the way to this point of the book without bringing up race, mostly because it shouldn't be an issue worth discussing. As mentioned in the beginning, every dad who ever lived, is living, or will live falls into one of three categories: Daddies Doin' Nothing, Daddies Doin' Something, and Daddies Doin' Work. Never once was skin color or race talked about, because shitty dads, mediocre dads, and exceptional dads come from all racial backgrounds.

Unfortunately, it would be naïve of me to assume others feel the same way. Race absolutely is an issue for many people today, and based on how some ethnic dads are portrayed, it makes the lives of some Daddies Doin' Work more frustrating than it needs to be.

When Emiko was about six months old, I remember watching a cop drama where a black man was arrested for some reason I can't remember. The detective asked the man if he had children and he responded by rolling his eyes and blurting, "Yes." When asked how many kids he had, the man scratched his head and said, "I don't know. Six? Maybe seven? Maybe eight?" The detective incredulously asked, "How can you NOT know?" And that's when the money shot came:

"Hey, I'm just having fun spreading my seed around town, ya feel me? I'm not worried about that stuff."

That stuff? The "stuff" referring to how many children you have? The little ones who depend on a dad for guidance, love, and support? Is that the *stuff* you're referring to, jackass? I was in shock, I became angry, and I wanted to reach through the television screen to shake the stupid out of this fool.

Then I realized something. This isn't real. The black man in this drama is a well-compensated actor playing a role on television. If he has kids, he probably knows how many of them he has, and he's more focused upon raising them correctly than "spreading his seed around town." Like a leaky tire, the anger began to slowly dissipate out of my body.

Then I realized something else. Somewhere, there are people watching that bullshit unfold on television who think all black men behave this way with their kids. They'll think black men are nothing more than gangsta rappin', dope dealin', pants saggin' losers who offer zero value to their families or to society as a whole. You, of course, know better or else you wouldn't be reading a book about fatherhood written by a black man. But don't be fooled, even in this day and age, there are more people than you think who subscribe to these beliefs.

The days of mouth-breathing numbskulls in white hooded

robes burning crosses in front lawns are over, but the Internet changed the game when it comes to racism. Visit almost any popular website that shares stories about men of color and more than likely you'll come across someone spewing something bigoted. Why? Because in this day and age, people can simply hide behind a computer screen and say whatever the hell they want without consequence. The scary part is that these people could be our neighbors, our coworkers, our weekend warrior basketball teammates, our book club members, or our kids' daycare providers. Oftentimes, we would never know that they harbored these feelings just by being around them; but behind closed doors, a completely new side comes out.

As a black dad who operates a popular blog about fatherhood, I receive my share of racist messages. But hey, it's not a big deal and I understand that it comes with the territory of being who I am. My main concern is, I don't want television, movies, and the Internet to shape the minds of our children when it comes to how some dads of color are viewed. The overwhelming majority of us are loving, involved, and supportive dads and spouses. But for some reason, the focus is on the Daddies Doin' Nothing of the world, and we have to change that right now.

CHANGING THE NARRATIVE

Quick, what's the first thing you think of when you hear the words, "Black Dad?" Don't worry, you won't receive any judgment from me no matter what you say, I just want you to be honest with yourselves.

Is it, "Deadbeat?" "Multiple children with multiple

women?" "Not involved?" or "Irresponsible?" If that's the case, you probably have watched too many cop dramas like the one I described previously. That's okay, because it's time to change paradigms as if they are poopy diapers on a fussy infant.

According to a recent study by the National Center for Health Statistics, among dads who lived with young children, 70% of black dads said they took part in normal parenting tasks every day, namely, bathing, changing diapers, feeding, and getting their kids dressed. Comparatively, 60% of white fathers said they did the same thing on a daily basis. Does that mean black dads are better than white dads? Of course, not. It's not about who's *better*; it's about realizing that the vast majority of black dads in America fall into the Daddy Doin' Work category.

But we never hear about them. Until now.

I have two brothers, and before I became a dad, I witnessed how my siblings always put the needs of their kids first. I witnessed how they never expected or wanted their wives to take the brunt of the parenting duties. I witnessed how spending time with their kids was always the most important and rewarding part of each day for them. Truth be told, I couldn't ask for better fatherhood mentors than my two brothers.

On another note, all of my black male friends with children are the same way. When I took some time to think about it thoroughly, I couldn't come up a name of one black dad I know who's a Daddy Doin' Nothing. What's more, I can't think of a black dad I know who's even a Daddy Doin' Something. Every black dad I know personally is a Daddy Doin' Work.

INTRODUCTION TO COGNITIVE DISSONANCE

Cognitive dissonance may appear to be complicated on the surface, but it really isn't. In layman's terms, it's that awkward feeling a person has when there is conflict between one's core beliefs and actions. For example, if a man commits to being healthier but still smokes two packs of cigarettes a day, he'll feel pretty crappy about it. In order to resolve the war in his head, he can either quit smoking cold turkey, or he can come up with various excuses why smoking isn't that detrimental to his health after all. No matter what he chooses, the end goal is to relieve himself from that awkward feeling as soon as possible.

Here's another example. Let's say you hold a core belief that all black men are deadbeats focused more on "spreading their seed around town" than being responsible dads. How you've come to that conclusion is irrelevant; the bottom line is, you believe this to be true.

Now, let's say you stumble upon my blog or this book and you see a black guy (me) who appears to be a great dad and loves his children. The same two things will happen: you'll either clutch on to your core belief as tightly as you can by making excuses for what you see, such as, "I bet he's a deadbeat trying to exploit his kids to become rich and famous," or you'll realize that your core belief is irrational and change your paradigm completely. In my line of work I see both occurring quite often.

There will always be a small percentage of people I'll never reach due to the color of my skin, and I'm fine with that. What makes me smile is seeing the reactions of people I *have* reached. Not a week passes when I don't read an email from a reader who thanks me for helping them change their perceptions about black dads.

Take a moment to imagine how frustrating it would be if you were really good at something, but a portion of society viewed you as being horrible at it for some reason you have no control over. That's the simplified version of what good black dads deal with on a daily basis. This isn't about whining over how "the white man keeps us down" or pulling out some mythical race card (whatever that means). This chapter is included to illustrate the unique challenges many black fathers encounter on a daily basis and how they deal with them.

Here are some stories from my readers to illustrate this point further:

Walk in the Park

Steve is a mid-thirties black male who works as a Project Manager outside of Atlanta. Here's his story:

> "During a particularly warm day, I took my nineteen-month-old son to the park so my wife could enjoy some much-needed girl time with her best friend who was visiting from Florida. While I was pushing him on the swing, an older white woman approached me to say, 'You're doing a good job and I really hope you stay in that boy's life. Young boys like him need fathers.' And without a blink of an eye, she walked away.
>
> I noticed at least two other white dads there with their children and this woman didn't say anything to them. Why did she feel compelled to approach me with her sage-like advice to stay in my son's life? Yes, I know why, but

that doesn't make it any less annoying. I love my son more than anything and I will always be there for him."

I chose this story because it's a prime example of the "guilty until proven innocent" mentality that some people operate from when crossing paths with a black dad. Obviously, I don't know this woman personally, but I would bet that her comment wasn't meant to be malicious or racist. The problem is, she probably held a core belief that Steve, or any black man, interacting with his child was unusual; and in order to "make things right" in her mind, she offered up her two cents. Again, how she arrived to that point doesn't really matter. What's important is finding a way to change her core belief by letting her know that black men who take care of their children are the rule and not the exception.

Daddy-Daughter Day

Brian is a mid-thirties black male working as an entrepreneur in Southern California. This is what happened to him last year:

"My daughter is three years old and we both mutually decided to sign her up for dance lessons. Our neighborhood is mostly white, and when I arrived at the studio, there were two white moms ahead of me in line. I overheard both conversations with the administrator and everything was quick and pleasant. When it was my turn to speak with the lady running the show, I was asked if I had a job because, 'late payments are unacceptable,' and was told there was a waiting list for kids my daughter's age. I walked away in complete shock. I make $125,000 a year, so I'm pretty sure that I could afford the $110 price

tag for the lessons. I was hurt and angry, but at the end of the day, I'm glad this happened, because I wouldn't want to send my daughter to a place that operated this way."

I'm sure some of you reading that story may be thinking, "C'mon, this isn't the 1950s. Stuff like this just doesn't happen anymore." Man, I wish I could agree with that statement, but I can't. It does happen, and it happens way more often than it should.

THE VIRAL PHOTO

Remember the viral photo I shared in Chapter 1? A lot of people loved it as it opened up a healthy dialogue in regards to the role of fathers across the globe. On the flipside, there were some people who wanted to spit bigoted vitriol at me and my kids. One person said, "You should give the kids back to their mom so you can go back to selling drugs or your bootleg rap CDs." Another said, "A black man taking care of his kids? What's next? Am I going to see Bigfoot today, too?"

The racist comments also came from black men and women:

"There's no way he would care for those kids if his wife was black."

"Another Uncle Tom marrying a white woman. I'm tired of these niggas who hate their own race."

I'm not shedding any tears over this stuff. As a grown ass man in the public eye, I totally understand that people are going to hate on me. It comes with the territory.

However, a seemingly innocuous picture of a dad taking care of his two daughters—something that should be expected of *all* dads—elicited a response like that? I'd be lying if I said

I wasn't shocked by it. I asked myself a lot of questions when all of this went down. What if a white man named Joe Thomas had two young white daughters named Paige and Rose and posted a similar picture. Would it have "broken the Internet?" Was a large contributing factor to why the picture was such a huge human interest story due to the color of my skin? Why are we even talking about race in relation to fatherhood in the first place? To be quite honest, I didn't really have the answers to these questions. All I knew is that it was extremely strange.

As mentioned earlier, there are some people who will look at my brown skin and instantly ignore everything I have to say about fatherhood or anything else. It's just a fact of life, and most black people doing something positive in the mainstream understand that. Fortunately, you're not one of those people who feels this way. But I bet you *know* one of those people. They could be anyone from your best friend to your barber, and if you choose to hang out with them, you need to figure out why you tolerate that behavior. We don't want our kids to grow up thinking bigoted thoughts, so why surround ourselves with anyone who holds racist beliefs?

HOW CAN YOU HELP?

We've already established that being a Daddy Doin' Work is difficult. Being a Daddy Doin' Work as a black man is even more difficult at times, because we have the extra challenges of dealing with how society perceives us. Are there shitty black dads similar to the guy in the cop drama described earlier? Absolutely. The key item to note is that those fools are on the fringe. The overwhelming majority of black dads are loving, involved, and we take our responsibilities as the primary male role models for our kids very seriously. Again, I don't personally know any black dad who isn't a Daddy Doin' Work.

It's easy to turn on the television and see black men getting into trouble in a scripted or unscripted fashion. It's easy to read statistics that boast one out of every three black men will spend time in prison in their lifetimes. What isn't easy is to think critically and realize that most black fathers are the polar opposites of what's portrayed in the media.

Please know that the black men who are doing the right things in society for their families despise the ones who give them a bad name. Similar to how society wants to focus on the bumbling, irresponsible Daddies Doin' Nothing of the world instead of the dads crushing it for their families every day, we need to stop giving attention to the knucklehead black dads of the world, too. Let's celebrate the black men who love being dads. I literally know hundreds of these great black men, including my two brothers and my dad.

I encourage all of you to meet some of them, have play dates with these men and their children, and spend some time getting to know their families. In doing so, you'll find that they are a lot more similar to you than they are different.

And one more thing. Smack the shit out of anyone (figuratively, of course) who spews racist garbage about all black men being deadbeats. Stop watching shows and or movies that promote such a lazy and irresponsible narrative, and create a culture for our kids that's more inclusive than exclusive. We have quite a ways to go in order to bridge the gap between perception and reality in terms of black dads, but with your help we can get on track.

CHAPTER 18

"YOU CALL YOURSELF A REAL MAN?" STAY-AT-HOME DADS

WE COVERED THE DYNAMICS AND challenges stay-at-home moms experience in an earlier chapter, but what about stay-at-home dads? It's the same, right? Well, not really. This bears repeating: I'm *not* a stay-at-home dad, but for some reason, people assume that I am because I operate a blog about fatherhood. However, after interviewing a few of these men and after taking a month's worth of leave for each of my daughters when they were each approximately three months old, I learned a lot about what these men go through.

THE WONDERS OF THE INTERNET

One day I was surfing the Internet and I stumbled upon an article on a popular sports website that piqued my interest. It was about a professional football player who shared his passion for being a dad to his two young sons. It was one of those articles that makes you feel better about society as a whole once you're done reading it.

And then I visited the comment section.

When will I ever learn to stay away from the damn comment section of websites?!

Anyway, this one guy posted a comment about how the article made him smile because he's a stay-at-home dad and he loves hearing stories about men embracing fatherhood. At that point, the trolls came out of the woodwork to attack him.

"You lazy sack of shit. Why don't you get a real job?"

"Does it make you feel like less of a man that your woman is making all of the money while you play dolls with your kids? Well, it should."

"LOL, what a pussy. And you call yourself a real man? I bet you pee sitting down."

I was floored. Granted, I probably shouldn't have been floored, because the KQ (Knucklehead Quotient) of website comment sections are pretty high, but I was shocked to learn that there are people who actually feel this way. In my mind, nothing is cooler or manlier than a dude willing to give up his career to raise his children.

In my world, I worked at my corporate job because I *had* to in order to get the bills paid. Don't get me wrong, I enjoyed my job, but if given the opportunity to stay at home with my girls, I would've taken it in a heartbeat. I understand that there are men who choose to work outside of the home and still are amazing dads, but all things being equal, I'd choose the kids over the cubicle any day.

A WHOLE NEW WORLD

The thought of a dude staying at home with his kids while his wife worked a full-time job as the sole breadwinner would've made peoples' heads explode as recently as twenty or thirty years ago. But the game has completely changed now. More women are college educated and have advanced degrees, thus landing them jobs where they can make more money than ever before. If a family with young children can afford to live off of one salary, it would be almost silly to not have the individual making less money stay at home with the kids. In the past, that person was always the mom. Nowadays it's not uncommon to see moms making more money than their spouses; and if it works for their families, the dad stays at home.

Jill, a corporate hotshot living outside of Seattle, explains how this worked for her and her family:

> *"Last year, when our daughter was born, I was working at a law firm making $165,000 a year. My husband was an elementary school teacher making considerably less money, so we made the joint decision to have me work full-time while he stayed at home with our baby. It was the best move for us, because neither of us felt comfortable sending our daughter to daycare, and we live in an area where we can comfortably live off of my salary. My husband is an amazing dad, but you wouldn't believe the grief he receives from men and women due to his decision to stay at home. He takes it all in stride, but it makes me so angry. People are mad because a man chooses to stay at home and raise his kids? Is this where we're at as a society?"*

In some circles, yes, that's where we are as a society. Not only are people spewing hate at these great men, these men have to endure a lot of challenges completely unique to them. For this book, I needed more than just my small sample size of time as a stay-at-home dad to make conclusions about the job. With that in mind, I interviewed some of these stay-at-home dads to get a better idea of what they go through on a daily basis. Usually, it fell into one of the following themes:

Men Shouldn't Do This

The mantra that has been etched into society for so long is that men work away from home and women stay home with the kids. When that script is flipped, it's amazing to hear what men experience. Here are a couple of examples from some stay-at-home dads.

"My daughter will be eight months old tomorrow and I quit my job to be with her full-time while my wife works. I used to play poker with some of my guy friends on Wednesday nights, but their comments started to bother me. Every week they would make fun of the fact that I left my day job as an auditor to be at home with my daughter by calling me a 'lazy ass who watches bad talk shows all day.' The last straw was when I lost a hand of poker and one of the guys said, 'Why don't you call your wife to see if she'll give you more money?' I was tired of being the brunt of their jokes and I never hung out with them again. The sad part is, many of those men are fathers, and the fact that they can't see that I'm putting my family first shows how clueless they really are."

—Paul in Alabama

"I was out with my two-year-old son on a Tuesday afternoon and struck up a conversation with a random woman at the supermarket. When she asked me if I had the day off from work, I kindly replied by mentioning that I stay at home with my son while my wife works a corporate job. She looked at me quizzically and asked, 'No offense, but shouldn't your wife be home with your

son while you're at work? That child needs his mom.' At first I thought she was joking, but she was dead serious. She didn't think it was a man's place to be at home with his kids. It's one thing to have a man think that, but I'm shocked that a woman feels that way."

—Jack in Houston

To summarize, these men are getting crushed for putting their kids before their careers. Based on the level of hate and ridicule they receive, it's almost as if they're put in the same category as Daddies Doin' Nothing, which would be pretty funny if it wasn't so sad.

IT'S A LONELY ASS GIG

You know what a lot of stay-at-home parents will tell you about their jobs? It's a lonely ass gig. That's not to say it's unfulfilling to raise children, but let's be real; there are some times when engaging in adult conversation is necessary to avoid losing your damn mind. A lot of stay-at-home moms have the luxury of hanging out with other moms for coffee dates, play dates, and cool mommy groups. But what about stay-at-home dads?

Where are their daddy groups? Where are the other stay-at-home dads for them to hang out with? If you don't live in a large city like Los Angeles or New York City, the chances of finding these options are slim. Not to mention, some of the moms they come across aren't very excited about having a man join the crew, either.

Kevin, a stay-at-home dad in Missouri, knows all about that:

"I love staying at home with my two-year-old twins, but I really miss the adult interaction I enjoyed while I was working. Where I currently live, I can't find any other guys with young children who stay at home during the day, and all of the women I come across look at me as if I'm some sort of jungle creature whenever I approach them at the playground with my kids. So, in a nutshell, there are no men for me to talk to during the day and the women want nothing to do with me when I try to strike up conversation with them. It's extremely frustrating."

Not every woman is against men joining their stay-at-home parenting club. As a matter of fact, many women I spoke to would welcome a dad into their group with open arms just to get a man's perspective on parenting. Unfortunately, there are some women who are very territorial and operate with an "Only Females Allowed" mentality, and that makes it even harder for these dads to network and maintain some level of sanity between all of the cartoons, feedings, and diaper changes.

STUPID SHIT PEOPLE SAY

When I was home on paternity leave with my youngest daughter Reiko, I took her to an outdoor shopping center in Los Angeles called "The Grove" to enjoy a beautiful autumn day during the middle of the week. Reiko was three months old at the time, and she was one of those babies who liked to be held, so I took her out of the stroller and strapped her to my chest in the Ergobaby carrier. As I was walking with her, a guy stopped me and said, "Look at you babysitting!" Without hesitation I fired back by telling him that I'm her dad, not her babysitter.

Trying to ease the tension, the man quipped, "Well hey, I didn't say you were the mom!" Still stone-faced, I told him that I'm much closer to being her mom than her babysitter. At that point, he rolled his eyes and walked away.

I'm sure that guy probably thought I had a stick up my ass, but really I was just expressing my displeasure over a dumb comment. We've established this already. It's impossible to babysit your own kids, and if people had any idea how dumb they sounded when those words left their mouths I'm sure they'd never say it. In any case, I figured if I had this happen to me a few times while I was on paternity leave, how often does it happen to full-time stay-at-home dads? That's exactly what I asked them:

> *"Oh man, I'm sure that if I get called 'Mr. Mom' or a 'Manny' one more time I'm going snap on someone. Why can't society embrace a guy who decides to stay at home and raise his kids? It's like we're the bad guys, when ulti-mately we're doing the best possible thing for our families."*
> —Anthony in San Diego

> *"I had a woman approach me by saying, 'Well, if you don't have a job, it's probably best that you're taking care of your kids instead of smoking weed and being lazy.' Huh? At that point I thought the apocalypse was moments from arriving."*
> —Phil in Boston

> *"Honest to God, I was once told that my kids will be developmentally stunted due to the fact that they spend*

most of their time with me instead of their mother. What the hell? I'm their dad, not some psychopath. The things people say to me sometimes is completely mindboggling."

—Derek in Indiana

"Someone told me that I must be gay if I want to spend time as a 'homemaker instead of getting a real job.' I have no problem with gay people at all, but how does one make the transition from a man staying home with his kids to talking about his sexual preference?"

—Joseph in South Carolina

This is a just a small sample of the nonsense stay-at-home dads deal with on a daily basis. And ladies—if you're involved with one of these men, I'm sure he's nodding his head in agreement or he has his own crazy stories to tell.

HOW YOU CAN HELP

First off, embrace the fact that the population of stay-at-home dads is increasing rapidly by the day. These men aren't "pussies," they're not lazy, and they aren't losers who can't find "real jobs." From my own personal experiences and from the information gathered during my interviews with them, you're not going to find more confident, loving, tough, and passionate daddies anywhere.

If you see a stay-at-home dad at the park with his kids on a random Tuesday, go say hello, introduce yourself, flash a smile, and do whatever it takes to make him feel welcome. As mentioned earlier, it can be a very lonely gig for these men at times, and I'm sure they would appreciate the kind words and support as they navigate through parenthood.

Also, operate with a zero-tolerance policy against anyone who talks shit about them. If you think about it, isn't it insane that some people verbally abuse dudes who choose to be actively involved in their kids' lives? Aren't they the good guys? Why do some people think it's okay to ridicule them as if they're deadbeats? From where I sit, any parent who has something negative to say about stay-at-home dads is probably extremely insecure about their own parenting abilities.

By the time our kids have kids of their own, it's possible that stay-at-home dads will be as prominent (if not more so) than stay-at-home moms. Hugs and fist bumps to any dad who is man enough to ignore the haters and negative stereotypes to keep pushing forward for the betterment of his family.

CHAPTER 19

DADDY GOIN' SOLO: SINGLE DADS

BEING A DADDY DOIN' WORK is tough, and it becomes even harder when you're responsible for raising kids on your own. When it comes to single parents, the majority of the time the discussion is focused on single moms—and that's not surprising. According to a recent American census, in one-parent households, more than eighty percent of children live with their moms. But what about single dads?

By the way, if you're looking for me to discuss the elephant in the room, namely, single dads dealing with custody issues with their ex-spouses, you'll be disappointed. I'm man enough to admit that isn't my area of expertise, so I would be doing you a disservice by talking about it. However, I will acknowledge that both moms and dads have endured horrific pain and heartache in courtrooms all over the world, and it doesn't take a genius to assume it must be the worst thing ever. My two cents is that I always hope both parents put their personal feelings for each other aside and make the needs of the children the priority. Does that happen all of the time? Of course not, but it absolutely should. I know all of this is easy for me to say, but everything mentioned in this book is about doing what's right for our kids; and handling child custody should be the same way.

With that said, this is not a contest to determine whose job is more difficult between single moms and dads, because it's extremely hard for both parties. This is about how the job differs for the single dads who are putting in one hundred percent effort to retain their Daddy Doin' Work statuses.

DADDY DOIN' WORK AT WORK

Unless they're independently wealthy for some reason or work from home, the majority of single parents have to work outside of the home to support their families, and some challenges are unique for single dads. I spoke with one dad named Dylan who has sole custody of his two young sons, and he shared his story:

> *"Being a dad is by far the most enjoyable job I have, since I'm now doing it alone, it can also be quite overwhelming. Any single parent will tell you how there's a lack of 'me time,' adult interaction, and sleep. That comes with the territory. But for single dads, there are other challenges.*
>
> *"I work in mid-level management for a medium-size software company, and many of my colleagues just don't understand that I have to leave work at a certain time to pick up my kids from school. I simply cannot stay late to work on projects. Additionally, there are times when I have to leave work early if one of my kids happens to be sick. It's not uncommon to see my coworkers roll their eyes or talk behind my back about me being lazy or not a team player. But when a female colleague has to leave early for her kids, nobody says a peep because she's a mom, and*

*moms are supposed to take care of their kids while men
are supposed to work. Sometimes I find myself begging
other parents at the school to watch my boys for a few
hours just so I don't anger my bosses and coworkers, and
it shouldn't have to be this way. The most disappointing
part about all of this is that it comes from other parents.
You would think that other moms and dads would offer
some level of empathy for my situation, but it's rare."*

Of course, there are single moms who deal with the same
problems at work, but until the world evolves into a place
where men and women are viewed as equal parenting partners, men will experience this quite often.

LEAVING THE HOUSE

Tasks that most married parents take for granted are quite
challenging for single parents with young children. Making
dinner, eating dinner, taking showers, and keeping the house
clean are just a few examples that happen inside of the home.
But what about when it comes time to go outside?

Russ, a single dad with two kids, shares his experience and
he touches on something that was mentioned earlier:

*"Leaving the house with my three-year-old son and
eighteen-month-old daughter can be extremely stressful,
and the stress has absolutely nothing to do with my confidence as a dad. It just scares the crap out of me (pun not
intended) when I take my kids places that don't have family restrooms or changing tables in men's restrooms. I've
changed my kids on the grimy floor of men's restrooms,
I've snuck into women's restrooms to change them, and
I even changed them in an empty restaurant booth. It*

is absolutely absurd that in this day and age, establishments don't have family restrooms or changing tables in men's restrooms. As a single father, I don't have the luxury to pass my kids off to my wife or girlfriend—and quite frankly, I shouldn't have to. These are my kids and it's my responsibility to ensure they are cared for. So why does society keep making life more difficult for guys like me who want to do the right thing?"

To reiterate, the changing table problem is one big problem. I'm sure someone will read this and think, "Big deal. There are bigger problems in the world than this." Of course, there are, but this book is about evolving fatherhood, not curing diseases, or ending poverty or war. And honestly, when a baby or toddler is having a meltdown in a public place due to a soiled diaper and a dad has no place to change him or her, *no problem is bigger for him in that moment*, trust me.

Every establishment that caters to children must get with the program. In other words, if a restaurant has a kids' menu, it damn well better have a family restroom or changing tables in both restrooms, as well. It's already hard as it is for single parents, and when single dads have to worry about not having the facilities to change his young children when out in public, it adds extra stress to his life that doesn't need to be there. This is a ridiculously easy problem to solve, so let's get on it.

NEANDERTHAL MOMS

Since you're reading a book about evolving fatherhood, I'll go out on a limb by assuming you're not a Neanderthal Mom, but if you are, this section may be a little uncomfortable for you. These women are stuck in the stone ages when it comes to parental roles and believe wholeheartedly that men cannot and should not be raising children without a mother being present. Don't roll your eyes and dismiss this as a myth, because these ladies absolutely exist.

Don't believe me? Check out this story from Eric, a single dad with a two-year-old son:

"After my divorce I moved to an apartment on the other side of town, and my son became friendly with one of our neighbors' sons who was a few months older. Oftentimes I'd bring my son over to their house for play dates because they had a big backyard to run around in, and it worked out perfectly. However, one day my neighbors mentioned they scheduled an appointment with a financial planner on a Saturday afternoon and needed someone to watch their kids. Since our boys had a great relationship, I offered to watch them while their parents were away for their meeting. And that's when something crazy happened. The dad thought it was a great idea, but then his wife pulled him aside for a 'private conversation.' When they both returned, the mom said, 'I'm sorry, I know you're a great guy but I don't feel comfortable with you watching my son by yourself. I just don't think young children should be around men without a female around.' I literally looked at her as if I was the victim of a hidden camera show, but the lady was dead serious. Needless to say, I stopped visiting with them after that incident."

These women are out there. I even had the pleasure of speaking with one in the studio audience when I was a guest on a nationally televised talk show. The lady said with a straight face that she wouldn't feel comfortable leaving her kids around any man who's by himself. Of course, I had to regulate and tell her straight up that her belief has less to do with men in general and more to do with her completely messed up line of thinking. Neanderthal Moms make life extremely difficult for single dads who want their kids to be social with others.

SUPER DAD NEVER TAKES HIS CAPE OFF

Let's say you brush your teeth every day. Big deal, right? It's safe to say that the majority of adults we know take part in this activity. But what if people started to offer you crazy amounts of praise whenever you did it?

"WOW! You take personal hygiene to a whole new level! I love it!"

"Your breath smells like a spearmint factory! It's so awesome that you brush your teeth as often as you do."

"You quite possibly could be the coolest person I've ever come across. I just love seeing people who keep their mouth really clean. It's so refreshing!"

That would be extremely strange. To make it even stranger, imagine if those same people offered effusive praise only to *you*. That strange feeling would quickly escalate into becoming quite uncomfortable and annoying. Chances are you'd get pissed off and think, "Why are you singling me out? Yes, I brush my teeth every day like everyone else. Why is it newsworthy only when I do it? Enough already."

We've established that a Daddy Doin' Work never wants praise for completing rudimentary parenting tasks that moms can complete blindfolded, such as taking their kids to the park, going on walks, or eating out at restaurants. As a dad who is an actively involved parenting partner with my spouse, I take my girls out by myself quite often, and I know how much it bugs me when people go nuts in excitement when I do it. But I also know it isn't an everyday occurrence for me. For single dads, this is a way of life. Ninety-five percent of the time when they're out and about with their kids, they are the only adults present to watch them, and that can provide some interesting stories, such as this one from Brad in Los Angeles:

> *"As a single dad, I try to ensure that the time I spend with my kids is as memorable as possible. So one day I took my three young kids (ages five, three, and eighteen months) to the beach. I can honestly now say that I understand what life must be like as a celebrity. I couldn't enjoy my time with my kids without someone (mostly women) approaching me to say how amazing I am for being out with my kids by myself. One woman—a complete stranger, mind you—asked to take a picture of my family so she could share it with her friends. Finally I asked one woman how she would feel if people gushed over her for taking care of her kids. She shrugged her shoulders and uttered that it never happens because that's what's expected from her. And that's exactly my point. I'm sure these women mean well, but they're doing more harm than good."*

On the flipside, Tom, a single dad in North Carolina, dealt with feedback that wasn't so positive:

> *"I remember going to an amusement park with my two young sons and women kept stopping me to offer some bit of parenting advice. Everything from how I was using the baby carrier to the type of food I bought for the*

kids was under scrutiny as if I was a complete novice. I've been a single dad for years! I got this. Back up, and leave me and my kids alone."

Ladies, I know we covered this point already, but it bears repeating. If you or someone you know wants to offer praise to a man for doing his job as a dad, or if you or someone you know feels the need to offer unsolicited advice to a dad when he's out by himself with his kids, don't do it. Ever. As long as he and his kids are happy, healthy, and safe, just smile at him, take pride in the fact that he's enjoying some family time, and keep it moving. The best dads in the world don't want or need praise or advice from strangers when it comes to taking care of our kids, because it comes as naturally to us as brushing our teeth every day. Many of the single dads I spoke with shared that this was an extremely annoying part of the job for them. In order to evolve fatherhood completely, everyone needs to start treating moms and dads the exact same way. I can speak for most moms (single or married) by saying nobody does backflips for them when they're out with the kids, so why do it for dads? There's no good reason, trust me.

HOW YOU CAN HELP

Understand that single dads are, well . . . dads. They aren't zoo animals to ooh and aah over. They also don't want your pity, your unsolicited parenting advice, or any bullshit from coworkers if they need to leave work early to take care of their kids. In other words, they want to be treated with respect and dignity just like every other group of parents. Based on my discussions with single dads, many of them believe their lives would be infinitely easier if people took time to fully empathize with what they go through and didn't treat them like outcasts.

THE OTHER DADDIES DOIN' WORK

I wish I could have a chapter dedicated to all of the varying types of Daddies Doin' Work in our world, but this book would rival *War & Peace* in length. So let me take a moment to give props to the best fathers in the world (not the below average or crappy ones) who happen to be military dads, stepdads, dads with special needs children, gay dads, first-time dads over forty, first-time dads under twenty, disabled dads, and any amazing man not listed who endures his own flavor of parenting challenges and still kicks ass for his children on a daily basis.

I salute these men and I hope you salute them as well.

CHAPTER 20
DADDY DOIN' WORK NATION

BEING A DADDY DOIN' WORK is a badge of honor that only the greatest dads in the world can obtain. If a man wants to sit on the couch all day, be lazy, and ignore his family, he'll never sniff membership into the club. If a man thinks he's Super Dad just because he pays the bills, he won't get in either. This is a club for men who embrace fatherhood, men who believe in equal parenting partnerships with their spouses (if they are in relationships), and men who put the needs of their families before their own. In other words, this is a club for men, not boys.

Since I started my blog, I received countless emails from my readers who shared stories of great men who step up for their families—a few of them will be showcased in this chapter. If you're a woman who believes great dads don't exist, I urge you to read these stories:

Against All Odds

"The Daddy Doin' Work that immediately comes to my mind is my hero, who also happens to be my baby brother. Having gained full custody of my nephew who was then five months old, marrying a wonderful woman,

and becoming the father to twin boys and a girl, he has his hands full. Three years ago he was crushed under a front-end loader at work—flat—head between his knees in a space of about six feet, crushing vertebrae, ripping muscles, and stretching nerves and tendons. Although he was injured incredibly badly, he still survived. His biggest fear as he lay on the table in the trauma ER was that my sister-in-law wouldn't stick it out with him. That she would take the three boys (and the little girl growing inside of her) and leave him. That was his biggest fear, losing his family. Not the days, weeks, and months of grueling physical rehabilitation that he would have to endure—that was nothing to him. His fear was not being able to be the dad his kids deserved. Watching my little brother grow into an even more fantastic person since he became a dad has been such a blessing. The kids and his wife were his motivation during his weeks in the hospital, months in rehab therapy, and continuing years of healing.

"Today, he still walks a bit like a weeble-wobble (those egg-shaped toys of the 70s) but he does so to chase after the kids and give them the most normal and memorable childhood he possibly can. Having lost the ability to go to work every day like so many dads, he gets the joy of doing the little things all parents wish they could do throughout the day. He takes the time to make each child feel extremely important; he gives special snuggles, he takes the kids on trips to nowhere in particular just for fun, and he lets the kids ride on daddy's lap in his "race car" (mobility scooter) when they go somewhere that requires lots of walking.

"When I see able-bodied boys (not men) ignore their

responsibilities as dads, it makes me sick. Fatherhood is what saved my little brother. Watching his babies grow up was his motivation to improve when the doctors kept saying he wasn't going to get any better. He is a true Daddy Doin' Work and an inspiration to dads everywhere."

—Angela

The Stay-at-Home Daddy Doin' Work

"My Daddy Doin' Work is our rock. Not only does he take care of our five- and three-year-old kids while I'm working, he takes care of me in my home office by bringing me lunch, helping to clean, and just checking to see how I'm doing. Additionally, he takes care of his community through his counseling practice and the meditation workshops he provides. His entire being is focused on taking care of people. While for some (like me), his work might turn into resentment and become overwhelming, for him it gives him energy. There is nothing better than seeing him after a good day with the kids (and not all days are fabulous), or after he has a good session with one of his clients. Our home is filled with tangible ways he strives to keep us emotionally and spiritually healthy.

"It's not always easy though. He often feels isolated in his role, because let's face it, he's in the minority. There are lots of mom groups, not so many for dads. When he takes the kids out, people assume he doesn't know what he's doing because he's the dad. I always see him stop when there is a show on TV about the evolving role of fathers, so he can feel like dads are finally going to get the message that they are parents, too, and that he's not alone in what

he's doing. What makes him so special is that he doesn't feel like what he's doing is special—he feels like it's his job as a dad. And in his mind, being a Daddy Doin' Work is the most important job he's ever had."

—Cari

The Single Daddy Doin' Work

"My father, Brian, has been the mom and dad to my brother and me. Both of us were adopted as infants from separate families. My biological father left me for dead with sleep apnea. Brian adopted me, and there was a time when I asked him, 'Why do you love me when you don't owe me anything?'

"He said, 'It's simple. Because loving you two is the best part of my life.' Step moms have come and gone, but at the end of every day, our dad was always right there, brushing my hair, taking us camping, working full time, etc.

"Brian is a unique man, because not only has he raised me and my brother by himself for the most part, he also made numerous sacrifices and never complained. My brother is autistic and he's not the easiest to deal with. But my dad's patience, love, and kindness continue to amaze me. In a world where horrible dads receive a lot of recognition, I truly hope he gets some love. Not a day passes when I don't tell people how amazing of a man he is and how much he stepped up for us when times were difficult. One thing I can say is, he's my best friend and a true Daddy Doin' Work"

—Aubree

The Influence a Daddy Doin' Work has on Future Generations

"My grandfather adopted my sister and me when we were four and two years old respectively. He walked me to kindergarten, taught me to ride a bike, how to cook, and how to love. He never left my side. He became a single parent when we were young and still never skipped a beat when it came to us girls. He taught me about finances and pushed me to finish school. When I got in trouble as a teenager he disciplined me and let me know when I disappointed him. He was the daddy he didn't have to be.

"He will be seventy this year, and he is still the rock I lean on when I am having a bad day. He's also a great grandfather to four boys and two girls. He tells my sister and I how much he remembers us when we were little, and he reminds us constantly of how proud he is of us and what great parents we grew up to be; and I owe that to him. Because of his influence, I knew what to expect from a future dad and married a great man just like my grandfather.

"After being given up by my biological parents, I could have ended up anywhere, but my grandfather's everlasting love for me saved me. He has given me so much, and has never asked for anything in return. Everything (and I mean everything) I am today is because of him. He is a true Daddy Doin' Work."

—Ashley

The Ex-Husband

"The Daddy Doin' Work going above and beyond in my life is (drum roll, please) my ex-husband! He may legally only have our daughter every other weekend, but you would never know it. He never misses a game or school event; he's integrated her fully into his new marriage, makes sure she and her half-sister are equals, and takes the one-on-one time with her. Does that sound like "doing what you're supposed to?" Well yes, it does, doesn't it?

"The reality is, we live in a world where some men choose not to be involved in a child's life after divorce. His love for our daughter goes far beyond paying child support, and his dedication to being the positive male role model our daughter needs exceeds my wildest expectations. His willingness to co-parent effectively has made all the difference in the world for our child. Even though it didn't work out for mommy and daddy, our daughter knows she is loved, protected, and provided for by both of us."

—Jessica

The Tough Pregnancy

"My husband Iain looked after me when we were expecting our second son. I had hyperemesis gravidarum, which is a condition at the extreme end of the pregnancy

sickness spectrum. It affects only one percent of pregnant women. As I was seriously ill, bed ridden and unable to look after our son, he happily became the sole caregiver of our five-year-old son, Elliot. He juggled working full-time, did the school drop-off/pick-up, homework, after school activities, all household chores, grocery shopping, and walking the dog. He even had to contend with feeding himself and our son, despite me being unable to cope with any food smells anywhere in the house. And if they did manage to eat at home, they had to deal with eating their breakfast cereals while listening to the soundtrack of me vomiting!

"Elliot worried about his mommy being ill and going in and out of hospital. Iain supported our son dealing with the emotional impact and practicalities of my illness during the whole pregnancy. He worked hard to keep Elliot's everyday life as normal as possible, but he also went the extra mile. For example, when Elliot couldn't sleep, as I was in hospital, Iain traveled all the way to his parent's house where he stood on the front door step and phoned Elliot to wish him good night. But he also did more than that; he surprised Elliot with a bedtime story and a hug to help him settle.

"Iain is floored when hearing about other men not wanting to be with their kids like he does. I'm really lucky to have my husband as a Daddy Doin' Work who knows that being a dad and a supportive partner are the most important things he can do."

—Salima

A Black Man Raising a White Man's Kids

"Darian is the love of my life, my soul mate, and my rock. Through a previous relationship, I have two children, and biologically he has none. He stepped seamlessly into the daddy role on day one and has done everything a man should do for his children.

"The fact that Darian is passionate about raising my son and daughter without any question or a second guess is above and beyond in this generation. But that doesn't tell the whole story. The fact that this strong black man wants to raise a white man's children was amazing to me, but not to him. He doesn't view them as white children; he sees them as HIS own children.

"When he became involved, my daughter had just turned seven. Within four months, she was ready to call him daddy. I told her that was a conversation that she would need to have with Darian, because that's a big responsibility, and he may not be ready. To this day, I don't think I have seen a bigger smile on the man's face. It took a little longer with my son as he was battling the fact that he'd already had a dad and what it meant for him to have a second one. Darian stood back and let my son take his time. A year later, my son's dad disappeared as usual, and Darian was right there to wipe his tears. Ever since, my son rarely asks about his father. He calls Darian his lion, his protector. Now he calls his biological father by his name or nothing at all. We are currently saving to hire an attorney so that Darian can adopt both of my kids. He

reminds me every day that you don't have to be connected to your kids by blood to be a Daddy Doin' Work."

—Jamie

Teamwork

"Before we were expecting our daughter, I had heard all those jokes about moms doing "all of the work" and how hapless or useless dads were in the baby department. I already knew that this wouldn't be true as TJ is a husband who defies all of the typical husband stereotypes. Once our daughter Olivia entered our lives, TJ not only reinforced everything I knew and loved about him, he blew my expectations out of the water. I could go on and on listing how completely involved TJ is and what a fantastic dad, husband, friend, and partner he is. But allow me to just give you a glimpse at why he makes such a fantastic partner.

"Due to Olivia being born a few weeks early (and my anxiety as a first-time mom), our breastfeeding relationship was incredibly rocky for a few months. Olivia and I cried at almost every feeding, and both of us were determined to overcome the obstacles. Luckily we weren't alone in our struggle. Every time I would wake up in the middle of the night to feed Olivia, TJ woke up with me every single time. When I asked TJ why, or insisted he go get some rest, he would respond that he never wanted me to feel like I was alone in this, and that we would get through this together. It didn't matter if he had come home from a ten-hour workday and would need to wake up the very next day at 5:00 a.m., he would still wake up

with me. It didn't matter if I thought feeding Olivia in a different room would help change our breastfeeding mojo, TJ would set up shop with some blankets and pillows in the room with us to keep us both company. He always made sure that Olivia and I knew he was with us every step of the way.

"When I tell people about those days, people often tell me how amazing he is. I just smile knowing that I am lucky to be married to a Daddy Doin' Work and husband who relishes every moment of being a parent as much as I do."

—Melissa

Dads Can Change

"I met and married the love of my life when we were both relatively young, and shortly thereafter we had our first baby. We both worked outside of the home and I resented that I was the sole caretaker when diapers were dirty and the baby cried. Then all of a sudden a light switched on inside of him. I am amazed at the transformation a dad can make. Jack realized what a family was and that he had to be a part of it in order for our girls to have the best lives possible. In other words, he grew up from a boy into a man.

"He took care of our older daughter, while I took care of the baby. He totally bonded with the girls. As they grew, he would drop them off at daycare, pick them up and cook them dinner. I would come home and offer support in any way possible. I would bathe and change the girls for bed, get things ready for morning, and clean the kitchen. It

was exhausting, but we had a system and it worked. We were a team. Jack said having the girls was the best thing we ever did. I had my dream family. Two wonderful little girls who loved their parents, and a daddy who split the duties and reaped the rewards with his special princesses. It didn't matter if the task was pleasant or unpleasant. He did it all.

"Sadly, our family lost our hero a couple of years ago. All three of us are still stunned at the destruction of our family. I really don't know how single moms raise kids. I don't know how married moms with reluctant fathers manage. All I do know is that the years Jack gave the girls daddy time, daddy love, and daddy discipline mean everything to them. I also know you have to spend each moment in the "now" and not the "down the road." Jack never wasted an opportunity to take the girls swimming or biking or to the park. He used those morning drop-offs and dinner times to laugh with his girls or teach them something new. The girls keep finding milestones that they wish daddy could be there for—first day of school, birthday parties, plays and concerts. An involved daddy has more impact on a child than he ever knows. In life and in death, Jack was a true Daddy Doin' Work, and we miss him terribly."

—Katie

TEAM GROWN ASS MAN

I bet you know dads who are just like the Daddies Doin' Work described in this chapter. It could be your dad, your grandfather, your brother, your son, your husband, your boyfriend, or your neighbor. When you're around them, you probably notice how confident they are with their children. Sure, they make mistakes—we all do—but their confidence never waivers when it comes down to how they do their Daddying thing and the love they demonstrate for their kids. That's because Daddies Doin' Work are grown ass men.

Speaking of which, there's a noticeable paradigm shift occurring currently when it comes to what makes a man "manly" in today's society. As recently as twenty years ago, the "emotionally unavailable, bad boy" dad defined what it meant to be a cool and acceptable dad in some circles. However, with the popularity of social media, doors are now opened into the lives of millions of people, and behind many of those doors are men similar to the ones talked about here.

Dads are able to see other guys who take fatherhood seriously and say, "Hey, I'm just like him. It IS a good thing for men to change diapers, it IS a good thing to hug and kiss my kids in public, and it IS a good thing to be an equal parenting partner with my spouse. I feel validated now." Once the validation hits, these men walk around even more confidently than they have previously. They've always known that their spouses think they're amazing and sexy, and that their kids view them as rock stars; but now they know something else: *everybody* loves a good dad, because in today's landscape, good dads are cool. Yes, many great dads don't need validation, and that's great. But personally, it makes me even prouder to know that there are more exceptional daddies in this world than bad ones.

As always, Team Grown Ass Man for the win.

CHAPTER 21
THE END . . . OR IS IT?

WELL, MY FRIEND, THE TOUR is officially coming to an end. And after all this time we've spent together, you're ready to continue your own personal journey into evolving fatherhood on your own. In doing so, I'm counting on you to do whatever it takes to ensure the population of Daddies Doin' Work continues to grow, while doing whatever it takes to ensure deadbeats and slowly-evolved dads become extinct.

Speaking of the population of deadbeat dads out there, I have some bad news for them: their days are numbered. More women understand that it's virtually impossible for these guys to exist without their help, and now they're done enabling them. No more excuses. These ladies now feel empowered to stand up to the Daddies Doin' Nothing in their lives by saying, "No, jackass. It's not okay for you to sit around watching TV all day while I work, take care of the kids, and do everything for this family. Grow a set of testicles and be the man our kids deserve."

Women with slowly-evolved dads can now confront their men with confidence and say, "Your paycheck is nice and all, but don't think for a second it relieves you from taking an active role in our kids' lives." It doesn't matter if you're a SAHM or a business owner, don't ever let a Daddy Doin' Something convince you that his work somehow excuses him for taking an active role in his kids' lives. Sure, he's tired after a long day at his job. But guess what? You're tired, too! Does that stop you from taking care of your children and being there for them? Of course, not. As soon as a child comes into the world, every parent is in a perpetual state of exhaustion, and it's not mutually exclusive to dudes who work outside of the home. Not to mention, in the previous chapter there were stories of men working demanding jobs who were still happy and willing partners to their spouses and amazing daddies to their kids. Every woman in a relationship with a man should experience this.

Last but not least, women involved with the best daddies in the world will continue to show them love and support, and they'll never nitpick them for stupid shit. As parents, we know that a Daddy Doin' Work is the kind of man we want our sons to become when they get older, and he's the type of man our daughters will seek out when they're ready to settle down with a life partner. It may take some time to completely realize the goal of evolving fatherhood, but with your help I know we'll get there.

MESSAGE TO THE DAUGHTERS DOIN' WORK

EMIKO AND REIKO, CURRENTLY YOU'RE both way too young to comprehend what Daddy is attempting to do; but eventually, you'll be old enough to understand and (hopefully) be proud of your old man's message. Even at your current ages you probably know that I'm far from being a perfect dad or "Super Dad" because I make mistakes every single day.

Emiko, a few months prior to your third birthday we were shooting hoops and I lifted you up to dunk the basketball. Being the numbskull that I am, I subsequently banged your mouth on the rim on the way down leaving your lips completely bloody and swollen (luckily, all of your teeth were still attached to your face). After a completely understandable meltdown on your part, you came over to me when I sat with my head in my hands to hug me and say, "It's okay, Daddy." I'll never forget that.

Reiko, when you were about six months old, we were running late to an event and I pinched one of your chubby little thighs between the car seat buckle and you let out one of your silent cries. Parents, you know what that "silent cry" is. It's when your baby is so upset and looks at you with her eyes and mouth completely wide open for about seven seconds before the tears and screams make an appearance. It wasn't pretty, but after holding you and throwing silly faces in your direction for about ten minutes, you finally started giggling to let me know you were going to be just fine. Yes we were thirty minutes late, but I couldn't care less. You were happy and that's all that mattered. I'll never forget days like that as well.

Throughout the years, I know that I'll continue to make mistakes like these. As a matter of fact, when I'm alone with my thoughts I always find myself wondering if I'm the best dad I can be for you both. I wonder if you're happy. I wonder if you love me a fraction of the amount I love you. Am I doing too much? Not enough? It literally keeps me up at night. It's my insecurity and fear that makes it so I never take a moment with you for granted. I have so many regrets in my life, but I will do whatever is humanly possible to ensure I have no regrets when it comes to our relationship.

I will *always* be there for you. You need advice? Daddy will be there. You need discipline? Daddy will be there. You need a dance party partner? Daddy will be there. You need a hug or a kiss? Daddy will be there. You're going on a date with a boy? Daddy will be there with his Louisville slugger to ensure that boy keeps his hands to himself. I'm kidding (not really).

Speaking of dating, I know it's going to happen eventually. I want you both to know that you deserve the best men possible to raise your future children. Yes, I'm a work in progress, but if you marry men who love and cherish being a dad to your kids as much I do with you, then I will be extremely pleased. The wonderful thing about all this is if my objectives are met, there will be a lot more good men to choose from in the world. Parents reading this book right now are raising their boys to be gentlemen who will honor, respect, and cherish the women they partner with. They'll teach their daughters to be demanding when it comes to what they expect from a man, and when they find good men, they'll treat them with equal respect and love.

Before you arrived into my life, I honestly thought I knew what love was all about; and I'll tell you straight up that I had no clue until I held you both. Nothing could have prepared me for the unbridled joy that comes from being your daddy. Absolutely nothing. If I could bottle and sell the feeling I receive when you hug me, smile at me, or tell me you love me, I'd be a billionaire.

Thank you, God, for choosing me to keep doin' work for my lovely, smart, spunky, and incredibly awesome daughters.

ACKNOWLEDGEMENTS

There's no chance of this book being in your hands right now without receiving an inordinate amount of support, guidance, and love from the following people:

I must start with my wife, Mari Richards. You deserve all of the credit in the world for being a true Mommy Doin' Work to our daughters while I spent countless hours writing and traveling. I truly appreciate the sacrifices you made for our family.

My dad, Dr. Josephus Richards, for being my first fatherhood role-model. Dad, if I can be a fraction of the dad to my kids that you were (and still are) to me, then my kids will be very lucky.

My mom, Laura Richards, for being my rock. Mom, you are simply one of the most amazing people on the planet. I know I drove you nuts when I was a kid, but I hope you can read these words, smile, and feel a sense of pride similar to the sense of pride I have from being raised by you.

My older brother, Femi Richards, for being the first of my siblings to be a dad and introducing me to modern fatherhood. Femi, I marveled at how you would come home after working grueling twevw-hour days at your law firm to be an actively involved daddy. I know you're a Harvard graduate, but no Ivy League education prepares people for how to be the best big brother a guy could ask for.

My close friends. There's no way that I can list all of you here, but you know who you are. You're the ones I confide in. You're the ones who know exactly what I've dealt with to get to this point. You're the ones who told me to keep the eyes on the prize no matter what. Thank you so much for being there for me.

My extended family, both near and far for offering love and

support for my dream. I appreciate all of you, especially my in-laws, Neil and Nancy Edwards.

The team at Jolly Fish Press, namely Kirk Cunningham and Christopher Loke, for guiding a clueless first-time author through the crazy world of becoming published. Both of you are incredibly professional, extremely intelligent, and damn cool—a rarity, as far as I'm concerned. Thank you for keeping your patience with me.

My superstar literary agent, Frances Black. You took a chance on me when nobody knew who I was and we've made one hell of a team since then. You are my voice of reason, my therapist, my cheerleader, and my friend. I couldn't ask for a better person to represent me.

My twin brother and best friend, Shola Richards. I could write an entire book outlining how important you are to me and it still wouldn't be enough. Nobody on the planet knows me better than you know me, and sometimes I think you know me better than I know myself. I remember when I doubted myself, haters laughed at me, and literary agents ignored me, and you smiled, "You *will* be a published author. I know it. We'll celebrate with drinks once your book is on the shelves." Well, the first round is on me, twin. There's no chance in hell I'd be here without you. Know that.

Last, but certainly not least—I want to acknowledge my amazing SDW (Subscribers Doin' Work). Your support, your emails, your humor, and your sheer awesomeness kept me going when I felt like I was spinning my wheels. It makes me smile to know you have the same passion to evolve fatherhood and make it cool again. I cannot thank you enough for the value you bring to my life every day.

Keep Doin' Work.

DOYIN (pronounced "doe-ween") RICHARDS is a father, husband, writer, Daddy Consultant, and public speaker, inspiring new mothers and fathers to think, laugh, and learn while evolving as parents and couples. He authors the popular and well-respected parenting blog *Daddy Doin' Work;* and since creating the blog in June 2012, it has rapidly grown in readership with no signs of slowing down. Doyin has appeared on national and international television several times, and is a regular contributor to Huffington Post. He currently resides in Los Angeles with his wife and two young daughters.

Follow Doyin at www.daddydoinwork.com